# THE PSYCHOLOGY OF NOTORIOUS SERIAL KILLERS

## THE INTERSECTION OF PERSONALITY THEORY AND THE DARKEST MINDS OF OUR TIME

# THE PSYCHOLOGY OF NOTORIOUS SERIAL KILLERS

## THE INTERSECTION OF
## PERSONALITY THEORY AND
## THE DARKEST MINDS OF OUR TIME

### Todd Grande, PhD

UNHOOKED BOOKS
*Independent Publishers since 2011*
an imprint of High Conflict Institute Press
Scottsdale, Arizona

**Publisher's Note**
This publication is designed to provide accurate and authoritative information about the subject matters covered. It is sold with the understanding that neither the author nor publisher are rendering mental health, medical, legal or other professional services or advice, either directly or indirectly. If expert assistance, therapeutic, or legal services is needed, the services of a competent professional should be sought. Neither the author nor the publisher shall be liable or responsible for any loss or damage allegedly arising as a consequence of your use or application of any information or suggestions in this book.

Copyright ©2021 by Todd Grande

Unhooked Books, an imprint of High Conflict Institute Press
7701 E. Indian School Rd., Ste. F
Scottsdale, AZ 85251
www.unhookedbooks.com

ISBN (print): 978-1950057252
ISBN (ebook): 978-1950057269
Cover design by Julian León, The Missive
Interior Design by Jeffrey Fuller, Shelfish
Library of Congress Number: 2020946599

*For all mental health professionals
who don't shy away from
the tough cases.*

# Contents

# Introduction

Years before I was a licensed mental health counselor, I developed an interest in unusual human behavior. I wanted to know why people chose to act in certain ways, what motivated them to maintain behavior, and what could lead them onto the road to recovery from destructive patterns. One of the most fascinating behaviors is serial homicide. Like so many, I read a number of articles and books on myriad notorious serial killers. Their behavior was inexplicable, disorganized, and malicious. What could possibly motivate somebody to conduct serial homicides?

As I moved forward in my education, I continued to study this aberrant behavior. Even though the topic was fascinating I could not commit a tremendous amount of time to write about serial killers because I was working on my Ph.D. in counselor education and supervision, actively treating clients as a counselor, supervising counselors, and conducting various consultations.

When I would have a moment to read about psychopathy, narcissism, sadism, and other traits related to serial homicide, I would record various insights that had occurred to me. Over the course of several years, I became better at memorializing these notes digitally and storing them someplace where I could retrieve them at a later date. This system was enhanced when I started creating YouTube videos about serial killers. For every video I produced, regardless of the topic, I would create an outline with a mixture of various talking points and verbatim scripts. As I continued to grow my YouTube channel my outlines were populated with almost entirely verbatim text.

Shortly after I started doing this, I realized that each of my outlines was essentially a book chapter. I had always wanted to write books on serial killers as well as several other topics related to mental health and personality, so I decided to construct this book using selected outlines combined with other insights I have had about these killers throughout the years.

Over the course of several months, I built a hierarchy of the various ideas related to the mental health, personality, motivation, and types of serial killers. From this book schematic, I was able to arrange all of the chapters, format them for use in a book, and add my other ideas to complete this text.

My own personality both facilitated and slowed the completion of this book. On the plus side, I tend to be high in openness to experience, conscientious, and low in extraversion, which helped me to be creative, diligent, and apply good analytical skills. The same high conscientiousness that made the process move quickly also applied the brakes as I wanted to make sure that my analyses demonstrated a consistent application of scientific principles.

The fields of mental health counseling and other related fields like psychology and social work are not always known for their scientific rigor. A popular conceptualization is these are *soft sciences*, which contain research that technically follows the scientific method, but still does not elucidate the topics with the type of clarity we see in other fields like chemistry or physics. This type of thinking allows myriad speculation and unsupported conceptualizations to creep into many narratives about topics like serial killers. To the extent possible, I tried to reduce the inclusion of material that may drift quite a distance away from empirically supported principles. In this framework, I tried to offer insights that are new, informed by science, and logical.

Learning about serial killers can lead to the development of skills in a number of areas including but not limited to personality theory, abnormal behavior, emotional regulation, and cognition. Through the study of these killer's extreme behavior, all behavior becomes a little bit more understandable. All human behavior is on a continuum, therefore, even though there are relatively few serial killers, there are many people who have various characteristics of serial homicide offenders like the tendency to manipulate, a sense of entitlement, grandiosity, impulsivity, and a lack of empathy.

I hope that through reading this book, you learn not only about serial killers but more about the human condition in general.

# SECTION 1

## CHAPTER 1

# The Minds of Killers

This book explores personality theory as it applies to most notorious serial killers in recent history. The science of personality theory has advanced dramatically in recent years and has cleared the way for this useful and edifying speculation about the inner workings of horrific serial killers. This book will answer several questions:

- What drives a serial killer?
- How does sexual desire fit into the motivation of a serial killer?
- Why do some serial killers stop killing while others escalate?
- What are the different types of serial killers based on personality theory?

These questions will be answered through an exploration of over a dozen modern serial killers.

Although serial killers have existed just about as long as human society itself, interest in this particular type of homicide offender has increased markedly since the 1970s. The rise in interest started with a few serial killers who were active in that decade namely, Ted Bundy, Ed Kemper (Co-ed Killer), David Berkowitz (Son of Sam), and Kenneth Bianchi (Hillside Strangler).

As time moved on, serial killers continued to emerge and fascinated people in the same way as the killers from the 1970s and in new ways. Richard Ramirez (Night Stalker) shocked people with his extreme and erratic violence as he terrorized California during a spree of killing and rape. Citizens in the area bought guns, alarm systems, and dogs, worried that they would be the next victims of this ruthless and unpredictable killer.

The boldness of Rodney Alcala (Dating Game Killer) as he hid not only in plain sight but on *The Dating Game* amazed people who thought that a serial killer would be easy to spot. As it turns out, he won *The Dating Game,* and the young woman who selected him was immediately overtaken by feelings of disgust. She would end up rejecting him and the two would never go out for a date, which was quite fortunate for her as Rodney Alcala had not reached the end of his murderous career.

Even though some killers like Richard Kuklinski (Iceman), seemed to be motivated in ways that do not conform to our understanding of serial killers, many killers fall into a familiar pattern. Kuklinski was unusual in that he was motivated by greed and perhaps a high level of vulnerable narcissism. That is, he was very insecure and could not tolerate any type of perceived criticism. This combined with his paranoia led him to be an unpredictable serial killer who acted out of rage. As terrifying and well known as Kuklinski was, he was quite atypical, as most serial killers are motivated by hatred of women and a need to dominate and control women. This desire is prevalent even among some killers that don't initially appear to be motivated by anything even remotely sexual in nature. For example, it is believed that Berkowitz was sexually motivated even though he used a handgun (specifically a relatively uncommon Charter Arms Bulldog revolver chambered in .44 special) to commit several murders and attempted murders against male and female couples.

## Structure of the book

I am going to describe the thought processes, behaviors, and feelings of several well-known serial killers by analyzing both common and shared personality traits and facets, as well as environmental factors that influence the development of these factors. I will also examine some of the more unusual and unexpected combinations of characteristics.

Serial killers can be divided into many categories; however, no classification model has been considered satisfactory. Put another way, serial killers are not easy to put into distinct groups based on their behavior, attitudes, feelings, thought processes, motivations, and other characteristics. I have decided to divide serial killers into four groups that divide them by their primary motivation, which is a useful albeit imperfect way to conceptualize these killers.

This book focuses mostly on the diversity of personality traits seen in sexual domination serial killers, and how those traits express in different ways and lead to various homicidal behaviors. This focus, of course, leaves three other types of serial killer, which I will cover in separate chapters.

Before moving into the various personalities seen in sexual domination killers, I will review serial killers who commit homicide for money, to advance a political ideology, and due to psychosis. After these chapters, there will be a chapter looking into the mind of the sexual domination serial killer, followed by chapters that will primarily review one sexual domination serial killer that corresponds to the personality trait of interest.

## Important Notes

**Note 1:** There is no single agreed-upon definition of what constitutes a serial killer. Technically, the old definition used by the FBI specifies that in order for someone to qualify as a serial killer, they must commit at least three murders at least one month apart. The current definition specifies two murders, but I typically do not use this one because I do not believe the evidence supports this low threshold as adequate to qualify somebody as a serial killer. For example, someone could commit a homicide in the course of a robbery and escape. When the police are chasing this individual over a month later, they may kill a police officer in order to avoid arrest. This would qualify them as a serial killer, but clearly, their behavior does not match with our understanding of this construct. Of course, the same thing could happen with three murders. An offender could commit a murder, a month could go by and the police could try to apprehend them, resulting in another fatality, and the same thing could happen again. In this rare situation, the person would not be truly a serial killer, but they would be captured by the definition I am using. Notwithstanding an unusual situation like this, I think this definition is sufficient to properly categorize serial killers as distinct types of murderers.

**Note 2:** Because most serial killers are male, when I use pronouns to refer to individuals who have psychopathy, narcissism, or have committed crimes, I will use he/him for the sake of expediency. It is worth noting that there are female serial killers, although it is not common and their behavior is typically quite a bit different than what is observed with male serial killers.

**Note 3:** Another important note moving forward is my reference to the Diagnostic and Statistical Manual of Mental Disorders throughout this book. This manual is referred to as the DSM and it is published by the American Psychiatric Association. The DSM contains a number of diagnostic classifications and it is used by most clinicians in the United States to aid in the assessment of mental illness. This means that more than psychiatrists use the DSM. It is used by Licensed Professional Counselors, Social Workers, and Psychologists as well as myriad other mental health professionals. It contains mental disorders that many people would recognize like Major Depressive Disorder, Schizophrenia, and Obsessive-Compulsive Disorder. The DSM also features many classifications that few would be familiar with such as Schizoid Personality Disorder, Factitious Disorder Imposed on Another, and Cyclothymic Disorder.

**Note 4:** The last important note speaks to the nature of speculation when talking about real people. In the mental health counseling profession and in other related professions like social work, psychology, and marriage and family therapy, professional clinicians cannot diagnose someone who is not their client. When a clinician makes a diagnosis, they are essentially stating that they have, to the best of their ability, identified a disorder by examining available evidence. The assessment that would lead to a diagnosis would include many components, for example:

- asking questions across many domains,
- gauging the style of interaction,
- observing the client's physical appearance,
- and in some cases, considering information from other mental health professionals who have treated the client in the past.

Even under the best of circumstances, mental health clinicians often provide incorrect diagnoses. With this in mind, it becomes even more difficult to diagnose a stranger, even if that behavior were ethical, which of course it never is.

Refraining from diagnosing real people is not just about ethics, however, it is also about logic. Why provide a definitive opinion when the chance that the opinion will be inaccurate is pronounced? Mental health professionals are permitted to discuss real people and events in the context of mental health, but their discussions must be qualified as not diagnosing and not offering definitive statements that cannot be supported by evidence. To put it another way, clinicians must explain the limits of the information that they are using and explain how they are simply speculating about what could be happening in a similar scenario, not speaking with precision about a specific situation or person. In this book, I am only offering opinions about what could be happening in a situation like this, rather than diagnosing anybody, including serial killers, whether they are alive or dead.

I think one of the best analogies to the distinction between diagnosing and speculation comes in the form of a man who has a friend who is an automotive mechanic. One day the man notices that his front tires are wearing an unusual way, so he calls his mechanic friend and asks him what could be wrong with the vehicle. The mechanic tells the man that he probably needs an alignment, but he cannot know for sure without looking at the vehicle. Frustrated by that answer the man inquires as to why the mechanic refuses to provide a definitive cause for the problem. The mechanic explains to the man that the vehicle may just be out of alignment, however, it could also be that the control arms are bad, the ball joints are worn out, one of the tires is improperly inflated, the steering rack is broken, etc. Until the mechanic examines the car, all he can do is speculate with the available limited information, which is insufficient to determine the exact cause of the unusual tire wear. In this instance, the speculation is not without value, as it educates the man to think about his maintenance of the vehicle, but the advice is not conclusive. Simply put, it serves a different purpose than a diagnosis. Similarly, this book is designed to educate people about mental health and personality. It does not provide diagnoses. Nothing in this book can be used to further the treatment of anybody discussed in it.

With many of the serial killers I discuss in this book, licensed and qualified mental health clinicians did provide a diagnosis under the proper circumstances in which a diagnosis can be rendered. Usually, this occurred after the serial killer was arrested. Often, when multiple mental health professionals conduct assessments, they come up with diagnoses that do not match each other. This stands to further illustrate the difficulty with any definitive answers in the mental health treatment professions.

## Conclusion

There is a lot of information that one should know before starting a journey into learning about serial killers, not the least of which are the mental health and personality factors that may be at work in such cases. In the next chapter, we will move from topics like the structure of this book and important notes to specifics about personality theory that will help us to better understand the minds of serial killers.

# CHAPTER 2

# Personality Theory

In this chapter, I review the overarching theory of sexual domination serial killer personality. Therefore, in this chapter, I will establish the fundamental information about personality, psychopathy, narcissism, environmental factors, and behavior necessary to understand the material in the next chapter. It is worth noting that the specific personality profiles of any particular killer will deviate somewhat from the quintessential profile.

In the world of mental health counseling, there are several models that are used to explain and measure personality. One of my favorites, and the one I will use in this book, is the Five-Factor Model (FFM). Also known as the *Big Five*, the FFM has a number of advantages over rival theories. It is complex enough to capture the nuances, like the types we see with serial homicide offenders, but also straightforward enough to be understood relatively quickly.

This model has five higher-level traits and six lower-level facets for each trait, for a total of 30 facets. To truly understand personality theory, one must understand this model at both the trait and facet level. I will review both the traits and facets here and will expand on the model as I move through the chapters.

The five traits of the FFM can be remembered through the acronym OCEAN:

Openness to experience
Conscientiousness
Extraversion
Agreeableness
Neuroticism

These traits tend to be independent, therefore if somebody had, for example, a high score on agreeableness, that would not necessarily give us any information about predicting extraversion or openness to experience. The traits do not tend to be correlated with one another. Facets, on the other hand, are positively correlated. I will offer a brief description of each trait and list the six facets associated with each trait.

A facet can be thought of as an aspect or sub-trait of one of the Big Five traits. In the FFM, each trait contains six facets. Unlike traits, facets are correlated with one another. For example, if any particular person scores high on the "self-discipline" facet of conscientiousness, they would likely score high on "orderliness" as well. There are, of course, exceptions to this, for example, there are many people who are high in the "friendliness" facet of extraversion who would not score high on "excitement-seeking."

## Openness to Experience

If somebody is high on this trait, they tend to be intellectually curious, adventurous, liberal, a flexible thinker, invested in theories, feel emotions intensely, and appreciate art. Low scores on this trait are connected to a failure to value aesthetics, the tendency to disbelieve theories in favor of what is perceived to be concrete, and experiencing emotions as dull.

Facets of openness to experience:

1. Adventurousness
2. Artistic interests
3. Emotionality

4. Imagination
5. Intellect
6. Liberalism

## Conscientiousness

A high scorer on this trait will be deliberate, punctual, responsible, and productive. Those with low scores are typically late for work, not productive when they are at work, irresponsible, and fail to think things through before taking action.
Facets of conscientiousness:

1. Achievement
2. Cautiousness
3. Dutifulness
4. Orderliness
5. Self-discipline
6. Self-efficacy
7. Extraversion

Those high in this trait are friendly, outgoing, and sensation seeking. They like to socialize, talk a lot, have difficulty engaging in deep analysis, and are assertive. People with low scores on extraversion are analytical, deep, quiet, contemplative, and favor environments without distractions, noise, or crowds.
Facets of extraversion:

1. Activity level
2. Assertiveness
3. Cheerfulness
4. Excitement seeking
5. Friendliness
6. Gregariousness
7. Agreeableness

High levels of this trait are associated with a trusting demeanor, being altruistic, complying with rules, and speaking in a straightforward manner. Low agreeableness is associated with valuing competition over cooperation, skepticism, critical thinking, and maintaining values under peer pressure.

Facets of agreeableness:

1. Altruism
2. Cooperation
3. Modesty
4. Morality
5. Sympathy
6. Trust

## Neuroticism

People high in this trait tend to be angry, depressed, anxious, insecure, and have difficulty resisting temptation. Low scorers tend to be cold, flat, distant, unfeeling, and nonresponsive to emotional stimuli.

Facets of neuroticism:

1. Anger
2. Anxiety
3. Depression
4. Moderation
5. Self-consciousness
6. Vulnerability

With this understanding of the FFM, the typical personality profile for a serial killer is a mid-range score in openness to experience, a low-score in conscientiousness, a mid-range to low score in extraversion, low agreeableness, and a mid-range on neuroticism with some high and some low facets scores. For comparison, the most socially desirable personality profile features a high score on every trait except neuroticism, where a low score is favored.

**FFM Personality Profile for a Serial Killer**

|  | HIGH | MID | LOW |
|---|---|---|---|
| Openness to experience |  | ✔ |  |
| Conscientiousness |  |  | ✔ |
| Extraversion |  | ✔ | ✔ |
| Agreeableness |  |  | ✔ |
| Neuroticism |  | ✔ |  |

## Psychopathy

Using this structure, we can now explore two personality constructs that are tied to serial killers: psychopathy and narcissism. I will start with examining psychopathy and then move to narcissism.

Psychopathy is a personality construct that encompasses a number of characteristics. Like all constructs in personality theories, psychopathy runs on a continuum. Many people in society are what we refer to as sub-clinically psychopathic. This means that they have a low level of psychopathy that does not impair functioning and in some ways can actually be beneficial depending on their career choice. For example, first responders, skydivers, and surgeons typically have higher levels of psychopathy than people sampled from the general population. Subclinical psychopathy helps people in these professions stay calm under tremendous pressure, which is critical to them completing their tasks successfully. When an individual has too much psychopathy, it can become pathological. This means that it does interfere with functioning. This is the type of psychopathy that is being referred to when talking about serial killers.

Psychopathy can be divided into two categories:

**Category 1**—called Factor 1 or primary psychopathy
Primary psychopathy is characterized by superficial charm, grandiosity, pathological lying, manipulation, lack of remorse, shallow affect, lack of empathy, and a failure to accept responsibility.

**Category 2**—called Factor 2 or secondary psychopathy
Secondary psychopathy is characterized by excitement seeking, parasitic lifestyle, lack of realistic long-term goals, impulsivity, irresponsibility, behavioral problems, and criminal versatility.

If an individual is high in primary psychopathy, they could be dangerous, but their tendency to commit crimes is usually based on weighing the consequences of their actions. They tend to remain calm during high-stress situations, which is consistent with low neuroticism. In one sense, the threshold for a primary psychopath to start committing crimes in the first place is higher than it would be for a secondary psychopath. The primary psychopath carefully considers their options without a great deal of interference from emotions. The difficulty of primary psychopathy is that when an offender with this type of psychopathy commits to criminal behavior, the behavior can be extreme and he is more likely to avoid arrest.

Secondary psychopathy is also dangerous but in a different way. A secondary psychopath is much more likely to commit crimes and more likely to do so impulsively. They tend to be emotionally reactive, that is, they have difficulty resisting the urgency to act caused by strong emotions. This is a result of their high neuroticism. Because of their poor planning, when secondary psychopaths commit crimes, they tend to do so in a manner that makes it easier for law enforcement to connect them to the crime.

Serial killers with primary psychopathy tend to be more prolific, more successful at manipulating people, and more likely to fit into a community. They may come off as cold, callous, distant, robotic, and smug, but people close to them in daily lives do not usually think of them as dangerous. Secondary psychopaths who commit serial homicides are thought of as disorganized, chaotic, reckless, and short-tempered. When people who know the serial killer find out what he has done, they're not surprised that he was capable of committing murder. They are surprised he committed murder because murder is so rare, but they also seem to appreciate that he was always inherently dangerous and unpredictable.

When TV crews talk to neighbors after a serial killer is discovered, one can picture a neighbor talking about a primary psychopath saying: "I never would've expected him of all people. He was the nicest guy. He more or less stayed to himself." The neighbor of a secondary psychopathic serial killer takes a different tone: "Wow, it's not hard to believe he would do that. He always was a hothead and boy did he like to drink."

## Secondary Psychopathy and Antisocial Personality Disorder

Secondary psychopathy is associated with antisocial personality disorder. The majority of serial killers who have been assessed by mental health professionals are assigned this diagnosis. No other single diagnosis is more common among serial killers, including other frequently occurring disorders like narcissistic personality disorder and schizophrenia. Antisocial personality disorder is one of 10 personality disorders listed in the fifth edition of the DSM (Diagnostic and Statistical Manual of Mental Disorders). In order to qualify for a diagnosis of antisocial personality disorder, three or more of the symptom criteria must be met (note: only a licensed and qualified mental health professional can make a diagnosis of this antisocial personality disorder or any mental disorder). I will review the symptoms paraphrase from the DSM and provide an example of how various serial killer behavior may have endorsed that symptom.

## Symptoms of Antisocial Personality Disorder

| | | |
|---|---|---|
| 1. Frequently committing crimes | Example: setting over 1,000 fires during the course of their adolescence and young adulthood | Berkowitz |
| 2. Pathological lying | Example: telling the relatives of victims that they died of natural causes, when, in fact, they were poisoned | Harold Shipman |
| 3. Does not think before acting | Example: often makes decisions quickly that are not indicative of forethought | Richard Ramirez |
| 4. Short-tempered and violent | Example: being involved in a number of bar fights | Carl Panzram |
| 5. No regard for safety | Example: breaking into the home of a married couple, killing the husband and sexually assaulting the wife | James DeAngelo |
| 6. Irresponsible | Example: getting noticed by law enforcement because they failed to have a license plate on their vehicle | Joe Rifkin |
| 7. No remorse | Example: being completely unapologetic through every phase of the criminal justice system | Carl Panzram |

In addition to meeting at least three of these criteria, an individual would:

- need to be 18 years or older,
- need to have had symptoms of conduct disorder before the age of 15, and
- not have had the antisocial behavior occurring exclusively during the course of schizophrenia or bipolar disorder.

## Narcissism

Narcissism is an undesirable personality construct that has been associated with a number of maladaptive behaviors including serial killing. Narcissism can be divided into two distinct constructs:

- vulnerable
- grandiose

Both types of narcissism are characterized by four qualities:

- self-centeredness
- a sense of entitlement
- need for admiration
- low agreeableness

Vulnerable narcissism comprises traits like resentfulness, distrust, insecurity, shame, hypersensitivity to criticism, defensiveness, internalized anger, and being socially awkward, distant, and unforgiving. There is no mental disorder in the DSM that directly corresponds with vulnerable narcissism. Borderline personality disorder would be the closest; however, there are significant differences between the two constructs that prevent them from being used interchangeably.

Grandiose narcissism is characterized by arrogance, social boldness, dominant behavior, self-confidence, superficial charm, being resistant to criticism, and being unemotional.

There is a distinct overlap here with primary psychopathy, namely the superficial charm and lack of emotions. This type of narcissism is associated with narcissistic personality disorder from the DSM. This personality disorder is notoriously difficult to treat and it is commonly diagnosed in serial killers. As was the case with antisocial personality disorder, I will list the symptoms of narcissistic personality disorder and offer an example of how a serial killer may have endorsed each item (may be found to qualify for the symptom). Five or more of the nine symptoms are required for a diagnosis.

**Symptoms of Narcissistic Personality Disorder**

| 1. Grandiosity | Example: a serial killer admiring another killer's work, implying that what they do is valuable | Gary Ridgway |
|---|---|---|
| 2. Fantasies of exaggerated success and power | Example: following women down the street and fantasizing about how they loved him and would never reject him | Ed Kemper |
| 3. Believing oneself to be special or unique | Example: believing it is their destiny to rid the world of undesirable women, a task which only they can achieve | Ted Bundy |
| 4. Needing admiration | Example: after murdering a victim, contemplating how people react to the news coverage | Dennis Rader |
| 5. Sense of entitlement | Example: being angry when a potential victim escaped | Gary Ridgway |

| 6. Manipulative | Example: talking a victim who had locked him out of a vehicle into letting him in the vehicle | Ed Kemper |
|---|---|---|
| 7. Lacking affective and/or cognitive empathy | Example: ignoring of victim's pleas right before the killer proceeds to strangle the victim | Gary Ridgway |
| 8. Envious | Example: killing competing criminals in order to steal from them | Richard Kuklinski |
| 9. Supercilious and condescending | Example: taunting the police as incompetent by anonymously communicating with them | Dennis Rader |

I covered psychopathy and narcissism as well as antisocial personality disorder and narcissistic personality disorder because they are frequently observed in serial killers. There are other personality traits (e.g. obsessiveness) and other mental disorders that are common in these types of offenders (e.g. paranoid personality disorder, alcohol use disorder, and disorders associated with psychosis like schizophrenia or major depressive disorder). These personality traits and mental disorders will be covered as they pertain to specific serial killers throughout the book.

## Are all Psychopaths Narcissists?

One of the great debates in the discussion of psychopathy and narcissism involves the theory that all psychopaths are narcissists, but only some narcissists are psychopaths. This false assertion results in the mischaracterization of many individuals including some who are serial killers. This is an interesting and expedient statement that's catchy, but it is not based in science. The reality is that psychopathy and narcissism overlap, but they are, in fact, distinct constructs that independently bring clarity to the assessment process.

To explain why this statement (all psychopaths are narcissists, but only some narcissists are psychopaths) is untrue, we must remember that there are two types of psychopathy (primary and secondary) and two types of narcissism (grandiose and vulnerable). This leaves us with four possible combinations of these two constructs; therefore, when addressing the issue of why all psychopaths are not narcissists, we are actually evaluating four statements.

It is quite clear that all primary psychopaths would not have vulnerable narcissism, as there are substantial differences like high versus low neuroticism. The same argument can be made based on neuroticism between secondary psychopathy and grandiose narcissism. This leaves us with just two remaining comparisons, which is the source of most of the confusion around this topic.

When looking at the comparison of secondary psychopathy and vulnerable narcissism, there are areas here where distinctions can be drawn. Secondary psychopaths are not necessarily ashamed of anything, distant, socially awkward, insecure, distrusting, therefore these constructs clearly stand apart.

This leaves us with the most confusing comparison: primary psychopathy and grandiose narcissism. Both are characterized by low neuroticism, grandiosity, a lack of empathy, and a tendency to manipulate. It is easy to see why this comparison leaves many people believing that all psychopaths must be narcissistic.

While these two are similar, there are a few areas of distinction. Primary psychopaths are pathological liars, whereas grandiose narcissists do not necessarily manifest this behavior. Grandiose narcissists have fantasies of power, believe they are special or unique, have a sense of entitlement, envy others, are arrogant, and require excessive admiration. Primary psychopaths do not necessarily have any of these characteristics.

Even in instances where a characteristic is shared, it may be expressed differently between psychopaths and narcissists. One of the best examples is pathological lying. Psychopaths like to get what they want like money, power, and sex. Narcissists lie so that people will think better of them, whereas psychopaths are generally not concerned about how other people feel. For example, a psychopath may tell a lie that actually makes them look worse if that will move them closer to their goal. A narcissist would not likely prevaricate (lie) in a manner that made people think less of them as that goes against one of their core drives.

It's long been recognized in the world of psychopathology and personality traits that simply the existence of behavior across two disorders or traits is not enough to make those disorders or traits the same. If one were going to use the *all psychopaths are narcissists* logic, they would have to agree that all people with social anxiety disorder actually have avoidant personality disorder. Even though these two disorders are often confused with one another, researchers finally determined they are truly distinct, because even though many of the behaviors are the same, the motivation is different. There is a clinical reason for the precise use of these terms.

If one were to make the incorrect assumption that all psychopaths are narcissists when they attempt to assess people with psychopathy, they would underestimate the number of people who had it because they would be looking for the narcissism as a defining characteristic of psychopathy.

## Environmental Factors

Now that the basics of personality and psychopathology have been illustrated, the next area to examine is the common environmental factors that affect many serial killers. When looking at a large number of serial killers, a pattern of childhood and adolescent stressors emerges. Serial killers tend to grow up in turbulent family environments characterized by physical, emotional, and sexual abuse, as well as isolation. Serial killers are of course typically male and they often have dominant mothers who frequently insulted them (e.g. Ed Kemper) or mothers who are quite distant and barely invest any energy in supervision (e.g. Richard Ramirez). Oddly, many serial killers were adopted (e.g. Kenneth Bianchi, Ted Bundy, Joel Rifkin, and David Berkowitz), but the evidence does not support some type of causal link. It appears to be a coincidence. Adoptions do not lead to psychopathy, narcissism, sexual sadism, or homicidal tendencies.

Another common, albeit surprising, environmental factor is head injury. Some of this increased incidence of head injuries with serial killers can be explained by impulsivity, sensation seeking, and other characteristics linked to homicidal behavior. Characteristics like these increase the chances that a child will sustain a head injury, so in this way, the serial killer tendencies may cause head injuries. This cause-and-effect connection is not insufficient to explain all the variance. It seems fairly clear that head injuries contribute in some way to future serial killing behavior. Many serial killers have had repeated and fairly severe head injuries (e.g. Arthur Shawcross [Genesee River Killer], Richard Ramirez, & David Berkowitz).

Just as certain environmental factors seem to occur frequently, early behaviors also seem to have a pattern when it comes to serial killers. Psychopathy has been tied to what is referred to as the MacDonald Triad. These are three traits that were put forward as predicting future psychopathic behavior:

- setting fires
- torturing small animals
- bedwetting

As it turns out, arson and harming small animals does seem to predict psychopathy, but bedwetting is not a reliable predictor. Several serial killers endorse the two somewhat reliable predictors of the MacDonald Triad. For example, David Berkowitz set over a thousand fires and Richard Kuklinski killed cats.

## Conclusion

Narcissism and psychopathy weave into the broader structure of personality theory and are overrepresented in the personality profiles of serial homicide offenders. Even though these constructs can give us insight into potential motives for these crimes, there are a diversity of possible motivations not only from personality, but from other external factors like comorbid mental disorders. In the following chapters, we will review motives like money, ideology, and psychosis as well as how they interact with narcissism and psychopathy.

# SECTION 2

### CHAPTER 3
# Serial Killers Who Kill for Money
## James Bulger

In this chapter and the two following chapters, I will review the personality characteristics of three types of serial killers that are not sexual domination killers. Here I will be starting with serial killers who kill for money and power not related to sex. The classic example of this type of serial killer is James "Whitey" Bulger, who was a notorious organized crime leader and murderer. It is believed he killed at least 19 people during his criminal career before dying in 2018.

## Background and Crimes

James Joseph Bulger Jr. was born in Boston, Massachusetts on September 3, 1929, the second of six children. His father was a union laborer who lost his ability to provide for the family after an accident at work resulted in the loss of one of his arms.

Bulger started his criminal career at a young age. He was first arrested at age 13 for delinquency. The police nicknamed him "Whitey" because of his blonde hair (it has been reported he did not like this nickname). He was frequently fighting and stealing, joining a gang not long before he was arrested for theft sometime around 1943.

He would be arrested many more times for increasing serious offenses like armed robbery. Juvenile reform schools held Bulger until 1948, after which he joined the Air Force. His low agreeableness would persist into this venue as well. He committed several assaults and served time in military prison, yet amazingly he was honorably discharged in 1952.

Bulger continued developing his criminal resume as demonstrated by his arrests for truck hijacking and armed robbery. This resulted in a 20-year prison sentence in 1956. He served three years at Alcatraz. Later, he would claim that while in prison, he was part of the MKUltra CIA mind control program and therefore used a lot of substances, including LSD. He was released in 1965 after only nine years and worked as a janitor and construction worker before working in organized crime, eventually ending up working for the Winter Hill Gang.

Bulger developed a reputation as a violent and clever criminal as he worked for this gang; therefore, not surprisingly, when the head of the gang was arrested, Bulger was promoted. He was extensively involved in all types of crime during his active years with organized crime, including murder, drug trafficking, arms trafficking, arson, loansharking, extortion, and bookmaking.

In 1974 or 1975, Bulger became an informant for the FBI, something that is highly frowned upon in organized crime. Bulger denies that he was ever an informant, saying instead that he made arrangements that look like he was an informant so that he could gather information about the FBI. Even though he was able to collect a great deal of helpful information from the FBI and manipulate them significantly, the evidence strongly supports that he nevertheless was an informant.

In 1994, law enforcement officers built a case against Bulger, but Bulger was warned by his FBI handler, named James Connolly, about his impending arrest and he fled on December 23, 1994. Bulger had prepared years in advance for this outcome and was in the possession of fake identifications and other resources to facilitate staying under the radar.

The FBI tried desperately to locate him, even putting him on the most wanted fugitives list but they did not have any good photographs of Bulger or his girlfriend Catherine Greig, who they correctly suspected was traveling with him. One significant break in the case came when the FBI was supplied high resolution photographs from a physician who had performed cosmetic surgery on Catherine Greig. After the FBI ran a public service announcement on daytime television, they received a tip from a woman who lived in Santa Monica, California, claiming Bulger and Greig lived in the same town.

The FBI started surveillance on Bulger's apartment in Santa Monica and talked with Bulger's landlord. On June 22, 2011, the FBI tricked Bulger into coming out of the apartment by having the landlord call Bulger and tell him that his storage locker in the garage had been broken into and Bulger needed to come down there to see if anything was missing. Bulger was arrested without incident. Amazingly, he had escaped justice for 16 years. The FBI searched his apartment and found more than $822,000 in cash, fake identification, and dozens of firearms. He was charged with 48 counts including 19 counts of murder.

His girlfriend, Catherine Greig, was also arrested and would later be sentenced to eight years in prison after pleading guilty to a number of charges including conspiracy to harbor a fugitive. She was sentenced to more time after she pleaded guilty to criminal contempt for refusing to testify before a grand jury.

After Bulger entered a plea of not guilty to all the charges, he went to prison to await trial. There he was treated by a mental health professional that he was able to manipulate into allowing him privileges other inmates did not have. This is an example of how serial killers can manifest superficial charm. The prison psychologist knew that Bulger was a murderer, yet she was taken in by his non-threatening demeanor and his desperate pleas to communicate with his girlfriend who he said he loved so dearly.

Bulger was convicted on 31 of 32 counts including racketeering and 11 murders in August of 2013 and sentenced to two life terms plus five years, although as it turns out the five years would have nearly been sufficient to capture the remaining time he had left. After serving time in a few different facilities, Bulger was transferred to a prison in West Virginia on October 29, 2018. The next day at 8:20 AM, Bulger was found dead. Bulger had been attacked by multiple inmates with a padlock in a sock and a makeshift knife, referred to as a shiv. He was 89 years old.

## Mental Health and Personality Factors

Many people believe Bulger's behavior aligns with antisocial personality disorder. He started committing crimes at a young age, he didn't seem to have any other mental condition that would explain his behavior, and his behavior was consistent for a long period of time. Looking at the criteria for antisocial personality disorder, there are areas that appear to align. Bulger repeatedly committed crimes, lied, was impulsive, demonstrated a phenomenal level of aggression, had a reckless disregard for other people's safety, was irresponsible, and lacked remorse even up to the end of his life.

All these symptoms are consistent with the personality construct of psychopathy. There are a few other characteristics of psychopathy where we see alignment as well, for example, he was manipulative and had superficial charm. One of the most fascinating examples was how he manipulated a prison psychologist, somebody who would normally be considered as exceptionally prepared to deal with manipulative behavior. Bulger also lacked empathy as demonstrated by his involvement in at least 19 homicides.

Some have said that Bulger was narcissistic as well. Other than the tendency to manipulate and lack of empathy, which overlaps with psychopathy, he may have also had grandiosity, sense of entitlement, and a tendency to be arrogant.

Let's take a look at a potential personality profile for Bulger's behavior using the Five-Factor Model:

**FFM Personality Profile for a Serial Killer**

|  | HIGH | MID | LOW |
| --- | --- | --- | --- |
| Openness to experience | ✔ | | |
| Conscientiousness | ✔ | | |
| Extraversion | | ✔ | |
| Agreeableness | | | ✔ |
| Neuroticism | | ✔ | |

## Openness to Experience: High

Bulger had an appreciation for art and liked to read books on true crime, which indicates intellectual curiosity.

Conscientiousness: High

Bulger was organized enough to evade law enforcement for 16 years. He was careful, deliberate, and even though he was committing crimes, which is an antisocial behavior, he was still technically hard-working. Usually, when someone is impulsive, we think of them as having low conscientiousness, but the type of impulsivity he had was more a difficulty in resisting temptation, which is measured on neuroticism.

## Extraversion: Midrange

This is a good example of behavior indicating both high and low facets scores. He was assertive and sensation-seeking, but not particularly outgoing, friendly, or talkative.

## Agreeableness: Low

Bulger was not trusting, which probably helped him to remain a fugitive for so long. He valued competition over cooperation, although he did cooperate with the FBI, but it was in order to more effectively compete with others in organized crime.

## Neuroticism: Midrange

Bulger did not seem particularly anxious but did have the impulsivity mentioned above, anger problems, and perhaps some depression.

Bulger's value system was quite different than most people in the population. For example, he did not seem particularly concerned with being convicted of murder but he insisted he was never an informant. He said that he made that deal to get information from the FBI, not to supply them with information.

There are conflicting accounts based on his letters and other statements about how he really felt about his criminal career. On one hand, he rationalized his beliefs like many who are involved in organized crime. He attempted to turn his wrong actions into right actions. On the other hand, Bulger appeared to express remorse in a letter after his trial to a few teenagers who wrote him for a class project, saying that his life was wasted and if they wanted to make crime pay, they should go to law school. In another letter he said that Catherine (his girlfriend) was the best thing that ever happened to him and his life would have been better if he had met her earlier, implying that he would have avoided a life of crime.

Bulger achieved antihero status through his manipulation of the FBI. A desire to embarrass law enforcement is a theme that we see across many serial killers. Few have had more success with this goal than James Bulger.

## Conclusion

As I discussed earlier, somebody like James Bulger would qualify as a serial killer, but his behavior does not align with the quintessential sexual domination serial killer. Here are a few items that distinguish his behavior from the classic serial killer paradigm:

- Bulger killed for money, status, and control over his own organization rather than killing in order to dominate or get revenge on women.

- He tended to kill quickly and use means that were efficient in causing death, rather than taking his time and experiencing pleasure throughout the homicide.

- His selection of victims was based on to what degree he believed they threatened him or represented an obstacle to his financial success, rather than due to the victims fitting some type of physical profile.

Even though James Bulger does not appear to be a classic serial killer, many people in organized crime who commit homicides follow a pattern similar to that of this criminal.

# CHAPTER 4

# Serial Killers Who Kill to Advance an Ideology

## Ted Kaczynski

Ted Kaczynski is an atypical serial killer, who was motivated by a peculiar anti-intellectualism ideology, the promotion of which in the form of a manifesto ultimately led to his arrest. Many have argued that Kaczynski was paranoid and psychotic, a theory that I will discuss in this chapter. Just as is the case with all the serial killers in this book, one can find a variety of motivations, each one operating to some degree. We are left to try to put those factors in some type of rank order if we are to gain understanding of serial killers.

Kaczynski would become famous for creating a new type of terror, one that could appear in the form of a package sent through the mail. He brought new meaning to the idea that no one is safe from a serial killer even if they isolate themselves from human contact.

### Background of the Unabomber

Kaczynski was born in Chicago, Illinois on May 22, 1942. Developmentally, everything seemed fine until Ted developed an allergic reaction for which he had to go into hospital isolation for some time. For several months after this he appeared fearful of separation from his mother, as well as less responsive and more withdrawn. Some experts believe this was the root of his later asocial and antisocial behavior.

In elementary school, Kaczynski was getting along with his classmates fairly well and generally socializing to a normal extent. His family then moved to a different residence and he had to transfer into a different and unfamiliar junior high school. At some point, he took an IQ test and a score was between 160 and 170, over four standard deviations above the mean. Due to this exceptionally high score and his general academic performance, he was permitted to skip sixth grade. Even though this was positive for him academically, after this he experienced difficulty fitting in with his classmates and was bullied. During these years people described him as shy, withdrawn and shutting down in social situations. He was referred to as a loner.

In high school Kaczynski continued to be thought of as an outside but he did exceptionally well academically, demonstrating a specific interest in and talent for mathematics. He added eleventh grade to the list of grades he skipped and graduated when he was only 15 years old. Kaczynski went to Harvard College and graduated with a degree in mathematics in 1962. During this time, he was described as a genius but retained his socially awkward demeanor. Kaczynski spent over 200 hours in a psychological study that involved him being repeatedly berated verbally and humiliated.

After Harvard, Kaczynski went to the University of Michigan, where he would earn both a masters and a doctoral degree in mathematics. In 1967, at age 25, Kaczynski became an assistant professor of mathematics at the University of California, Berkeley. In this position he conducted research and taught students. The students were not impressed with his teaching style, describing it as rigid and disconnected. His teaching methods included reading from the textbook, ignoring questions, and failing to interact in a meaningful way with the students. Kaczynski left that position in 1969, offering no explanation for his decision.

Kaczynski moved back home with his parents and in 1971 he moved to a 10 ft. X 14 ft. cabin that he and his brother (David) had built outside of Lincoln, Montana. His life there was simple, which was not unusual for the area. His residence did not have running water or electricity and he would ride a bicycle when he had to go to town. Increasing concerns about his ability to live peacefully swept over him when he considered the expansion of industry into the area. His criminal career would begin shortly after this.

Up until the point he was arrested, Kaczynski had no significant criminal history, no religious affiliation, no history of substance use, and a brief history of seeking mental health treatment.

## The Rise of the Unabomber

From the perspective of an outside observer, Ted Kaczynski's criminal career started on May 25, 1978. A package wrapped in brown paper was found on the campus of the University of Illinois in Chicago. The package was labeled directing it back to the sender, a professor at nearby Northwestern University. That professor, however, did not actually send the package, therefore that direction looked suspicious. He gave it to campus security and it exploded, injuring one of the security guards.

After this we see a string of bombings. In May of 1979, a graduate student at Northwestern University was injured by a bomb. In November of that same year, 12 passengers aboard American Airlines flight from Chicago to Washington DC were injured from smoke inhalation caused by a bomb in the cargo area of the aircraft that failed to detonate properly. This occurred when the plane was in flight and caused an emergency landing. In June of 1980, the president of American Airlines was injured by a bomb.

At this point the FBI formed the Unabomber task force, named for the earliest targets, universities and airlines. They had no idea Ted Kaczynski was the person for whom they were looking. The FBI discovered that the suspect used materials that were commonly available like nails, tape, fishing wire, and wood. They found neither fingerprints nor DNA. There were also false clues left in the packages, evidently designed to mislead investigators.

From October of 1981 through June of 1985, six more bombs were sent to universities, two were defused, and four caused injuries to five different people. In December of 1985, a computer store owner was killed, making it the first murder that Kaczynski would commit. In February of 1987, a bomb exploded in Salt Lake City injuring a computer store owner. A woman reported seeing a man in the parking lot outside that store, her recollection leads to the now famous drawing of the Unabomber suspect. In June of 1993, two bombs injured two more people, with the attacks occurring two days apart. One of Kaczynski's bombs kills an advertising executive in New Jersey in December 1994. Just five months later, another one kills a timber industry lobbyist in California. Kaczynski had murdered three people and wounded 23 from 1978 to 1995.

In June of 1995, Kaczynski sent a 35,000-word essay titled *Industrial Society and its Future* to the New York Times, Washington Post, and some other media outlets, demanding that they publish this manifesto. He promised that he would stop the bombings if they satisfied his demand.

## Investigation and Arrest

The FBI had formed a psychological profile of the Unabomber suspect. They theorized the suspect had connections to academia, was highly intelligent, and had degrees in the hard sciences. Interestingly, this was extremely accurate, but the FBI gave up on this profile a few years after it was formed.

The FBI offered a $1,000,000 reward for information leading to the arrest of the suspect. This, combined with the publication of the manifesto, led to the FBI receiving over a thousand calls a day for several months. One of the people who contacted the FBI was David Kaczynski, Ted Kaczynski's younger brother. David had recognized the style of writing as belonging to his older brother. It took the FBI two months of investigating this possible match to get a warrant to search Kaczynski's cabin located outside of Lincoln, Montana. Prior to the tip from David Kaczynski, Ted Kaczynski's name had never been on any list of potential suspects compiled by the FBI. Prior to this, agents believed the suspect they were looking for was 10 years older than Kaczynski.

Ted was taken into custody on April 3, 1996. The FBI found 40,000 journal pages that Kaczynski had written by hand, containing descriptions of the crimes and instructions on how to make explosives. They found a live bomb, which in theory was ready to be mailed, so it would seem that Kaczynski was planning on breaking his promise. In addition to all this evidence, they found the original manuscript of the manifesto. In 1998, Kaczynski accepted a plea deal where he would serve the rest of his life in prison. The numerous appeals he has filed have been unsuccessful.

## The Mind of the Unabomber

Kaczynski once said "Science has no business probing the workings of the human mind." It is reasonable to assume he did not have a particular fondness for mental health professionals, although he did get to spend time with many of them during his incarceration.

Let's take a look at Kaczynski's potential personality profile using the Five-Factor Model:

**FFM Personality Profile for a Serial Killer**

|  | HIGH | MID | LOW |
|---|---|---|---|
| Openness to experience | ✔ | | |
| Conscientiousness | ✔ | ✔ | |
| Extraversion | | | ✔ |
| Agreeableness | | | ✔ |
| Neuroticism | | ✔ | |

## Openness to Experience: High

His level of openness to experience was so high he was approaching psychosis. Kaczynski was highly invested in theory, fantasy, and he was intellectually curious.

## Conscientiousness: Midrange to High

Kaczynski generally had a good work ethic, was productive, organized, cautious, and had self-discipline.

## Extraversion: Extremely Low

Kaczynski was good at analyzing, shy, not particularly friendly, not at all outgoing, not talkative, and had few positive emotions.

## Agreeableness: Low

He was not altruistic or empathic, and he had an extremely low level of trust

## Neuroticism: Midrange

Kaczynski did not generally give into temptation, and was not emotionally reactive; however, he had feelings of anxiety and depression.

Ted Kaczynski had an amazing intellect, which was recognized early in his life and throughout his limited career. When he was in prison in 1996, he was given an IQ test and scored a 136, substantially lower than his prior score of 160 to 170, but over two standard deviations above the mean is still impressive. High levels of intelligence often appear to come at a cost. Many people in that situation are socially awkward, disconnected, do not like being around people, and feel like they are on the outside.

Kaczynski had a number of interactions with mental health professionals who formed various opinions about his potential psychopathology. When he was at the University of Michigan, he had fantasies of being a female, which was somewhat disturbing to him. He went to talk to a mental health clinician, but in the waiting room he became anxious. By the time he went in to see the clinician, he was depressed and anxious. In 1988, he sought counseling several times around the issue of establishing relationships with women and reported depression and insomnia as well.

Before he entered into a plea agreement in 1998, Kaczynski objected to the idea that he should mount an insanity defense, which was what his attorney was recommending. On January 7, 1998, he attempted to commit suicide by using his underwear as a tourniquet. When his vision became blurry and he started to feel dizzy, he worried about the possible brain damage he could sustain in a nonfatal attempt. His attempt led to a judge ordering a mental health evaluation. A clinician named Dr. Sally Johnson performed the evaluation. The total interview time was about 22 hours, an intake interview at a mental health agency would take about 1.5 to 2.5 hours, so this was an extremely thorough evaluation.

Dr. Johnson gave Kaczynski a provisional diagnosis of schizophrenia, paranoid type. This diagnosis was available in 1998 under DSM-IV. It would simply be referred to as schizophrenia in the current version of the DSM. In addition, she diagnosed him with paranoid personality disorder, with antisocial and avoidant features. When features are described like this, it indicates that certain characteristics of those disorders were observed in the client. She believed that the paranoid personality disorder was premorbid, meaning it existed prior to the onset of schizophrenia.

The schizophrenia was justified by the presence of two long-standing delusional beliefs:

1. Modern technology was controlling him, and

2. He was verbally abused by his parents when he was young, which led him to be unable to establish a relationship with a woman.

The paranoid personality disorder diagnosis was justified by Kaczynski's pervasive distrust of others. Even though Kaczynski's behavior endorsed enough of the antisocial personality disorder symptom criteria for a diagnosis, he did not have conduct disorder symptoms before the age of 15, therefore he was not given a diagnosis.

Ted Kaczynski's development into one of the most feared serial killers in modern history followed an atypical course. How is it that somebody who did not have conduct disorder symptoms before the age of 15 could otherwise exhibit antisocial personality disorder criteria like repeated criminal behavior, aggressiveness, a reckless disregard for safety, and a lack of remorse? There is no such thing as a late onset personality disorder. All personality disorders are thought to have an onset in childhood and early adolescence, yet Kaczynski stayed out of trouble when he was young.

His unusual presentation leaves us with two theories:

1. He had delusions that expressed as a tremendous distrust and hatred of what he saw as a dangerous rise in technology and industrialization, or

2. His paranoia, eccentric nature, social awkward-
   ness, and other symptoms led him to a delusional
   state or something approaching psychosis.
   Kaczynski was either psychotic or on the edge of
   psychosis, but either way he came to believe
   homicide was justified, leading to a campaign of
   death and fear.

## Conclusion

Serial killers are rarely feared outside the local area where they
operate, but Ted Kaczynski was an exception. His power to kill
and terrorize extended to wherever the mail service would deliver. This combined with his intelligence and ideological motivation made Kaczynski difficult to profile and apprehend. In
the next chapter, we will explore a killer with an entirely different type of motivation, but one who was nevertheless able to
inspire fear in many who became aware of the unusual nature
of his crimes.

## CHAPTER 5

# Psychotic Serial Killers

## Ed Gein

Ed Gein (pronounced like "green" without the "r") is one of the most unusual serial killers who has ever lived. Even though he could technically be qualified as a sexual domination serial killer, he is often thought of as a psychotic serial killer, driven by delusions that developed out of an extreme level of maladaptive attachment to his mother. Gein is the inspiration for a number of famous fictional characters including Norman Bates from the 1960 movie *Psycho,* Buffalo Bill in the 1991 movie *The Silence of the Lambs,* and Leatherface from the 1974 film *The Texas Chainsaw Massacre.*

### Background of Ed Gein

Ed Gein was born on August 27, 1906, in La Crosse, Wisconsin. His father, George, had difficulty regulating his intake of alcohol and worked various jobs. Gein's mother, Augusta, decided to move the family to a farm to escape what she perceived as evil all around them. Gein spent a lot of time on that farm, only leaving to go to school.

Augusta ran a grocery business and was the primary source of financial support for the family. She was described as having fanatically religious beliefs. She used to read passages from the Bible about homicide and death in general to Gein and his older brother Henry. Her view of women was that they were instruments of the devil because they tempted man into sin. She took offense at any reference to sexual behavior, believing that it was the root of much of the destruction of the world. Augusta imposed her beliefs on her sons with a fierce level of control and domination, restricting where Gein could go and who he could talk to. She immediately destroyed any potential friendships that Gein would attempt to form.

Gein's performance in school was within a normal range although he did well with reading. He was shy, would sometimes inappropriately laugh, and was picked on by the other students because of a growth on his left eyelid that impaired his vision to a small degree. When he would come home upset because of the bullying, George would beat him with such force and ferocity that Gein's ears would ring afterward. Based on the symptom, it is reasonable to believe that Gein may have sustained head injuries from these attacks. Gein would drop out of school in the eighth grade.

George died in 1940 due to his alcohol consumption. He was 66 years of age. Even though George did not contribute a great deal financially to the family, they lived so close to the edge that George's death placed Gein and his brother in a situation where they needed to take a more active role in producing income. They started working jobs in the community and each earned a good reputation as handymen. Gein also worked as a babysitter and felt as though he connected with children much better than he did with adults.

Henry became increasingly concerned about how close Gein was with Augusta, which led him to openly criticize Augusta, drawing the ire of Gein. This may have contributed to Henry's death.

In May of 1944, Gein and Henry were working on the farm and had set a fire to burn vegetation, a common procedure when working a farm. The fire grew too large and the fire department responded. After the fire was extinguished, Gein indicated that Henry was missing, yet was able to lead the authorities directly to Henry's body. Incredibly, even though Henry had bruises on his head, the coroner ruled the cause of death as asphyxiation. They believed that Henry inhaled the smoke from the out-of-control fire, leading to his death. Many in the community suspected that Gein killed Henry, but he was never charged.

Gein developed an interest in books about grave robbing, human anatomy, cannibals, and a few other topics that became disturbing to Augusta. Whatever she may have done to dissuade Gein from this material does not appear to have been effective.

In December of 1945, Gein's mother died as a result of a stroke. Gein was particularly close to his mother and his level of distress that her death was commensurate to his level of attachment. He used boards to block off rooms that his mother had regularly used, spending much of his time in the kitchen and a small utility room next to the kitchen. Gein remained on the farm, occasionally working as a handyman. Surprisingly, he was still getting babysitting jobs.

## Ed Gein's Homicidal Behavior

On November 16, 1957, a local hardware store operator named Bernice Worden disappeared. The hardware store's truck had been seen driving from the back of the store at 9:30 a.m. and the store was closed that entire day. A deputy sheriff, who happened to be Worden's son, went to the store around 5 p.m. After entering, he found bloodstains on the floor and he noticed the cash register was open. Ed Gein and had been in the store the night before Worden went missing as well as the morning she went missing, making him a logical suspect in her murder.

The police searched Gein's farm and found Worden's body. She had been shot with a .22 caliber firearm and her body was decapitated. The remains of another murder victim named

Mary Hogan were also found. In addition to these remains, the police would find even more disturbing evidence. A number of body parts and items made from these parts were identified, for example, masks made from human heads, chairs covered in human skin, bowls made from skulls, and a lampshade made from human face.

Gein revealed that he had made numerous visits to local graveyards from 1947 to 1952 and exhumed bodies while in some type of daze. The first body he dug up was that of his mother, after which he removed her head and brought it back to the house. On several occasions, Gein would use the obituaries to identify recently deceased women who looked like his mother and dig up their bodies. He then removed various body parts and crafted the different items.

Gein was also trying to build a suit out of the women's skin so that he could wear it and transform into his mother. Later he would say that he had strange visions during this time. It is reasonable to believe these could have been hallucinations.

Gein claimed seeing the bodies led to sexual gratification, namely masturbation, but he did not actually have sex with the bodies because "they smelled too bad." Even though he did not have sexual contact directly with the bodies, this behavior still qualifies as necrophilia and could lead to him being classified as a sexual domination serial killer.

Gein confessed to the murder of Mary Hogan, but later he would pretend he did not remember what happened. Gein was a suspect in several other murders, including Evelyn Hartley, who disappeared in 1953. It is believed that Ed Gein killed at least five people, although only two homicides can be attributed to him with any level of certainty: Bernice Worden and Mary Hogan.

When Ed was being questioned by the police, one of the police officers rammed Ed's head into a brick wall. Due to this illegal and coercive behavior by the police, Gein's confession was ruled inadmissible. Fortunately, there was enough evidence to prosecute Gein without a confession.

## Court Proceedings

In 1957, Gein pleaded not guilty by reason of insanity to one count of first-degree murder, but he was found mentally incompetent after being diagnosed with schizophrenia. He was sent to a maximum-security mental health facility in Wisconsin. In 1968, mental health professionals determined that Gein was now mentally competent to stand trial, and he was tried in November of that year. Gein had told a mental health professional who testified at the trial that he was looking at a firearm (.22 caliber Marlin rifle) in Worden's store and he attempted to load a cartridge into the weapon when it discharged, accidentally killing her. He claimed that he did not remember anything else that occurred on the morning of her death.

Gein had elected to have the verdict of the trial determined by a judge, waving his constitutional right to be tried by a jury of his peers. The judge found him guilty and a second trial began to determine if Gein was insane. After that trial was over, the judge ruled that Gein was not guilty by reason of insanity. Gein would be committed to a mental hospital. He filed a petition to be released in 1974, but it was rejected. Ed Gein would die on July 26, 1984, at age 77.

## Mental Health and Personality Factors

During Gein's time in a mental hospital after he was found not guilty by reason of insanity, he was reported to be a model patient. The staff never had to use medications to sedate him, he complied with the rules, and he took an interest in different crafts, like rug making and stone polishing. Other than staring at the nurses and other female staff, which made them feel quite uncomfortable, the staff viewed him as relatively normal.

Gein's potential personality profile may provide some insight into his behavior:

| FFM Personality Profile for a Serial Killer | | | |
|---|---|---|---|
| | HIGH | MID | LOW |
| Openness to experience | ✔ | | |
| Conscientiousness | | ✔ | |
| Extraversion | | | ✔ |
| Agreeableness | | | ✔ |
| Neuroticism | ✔ | | |

## Openness to Experience: High

He was intellectually curious, but not good at school. School had a social component that he could not adequately achieve. Based on his affinity for creating crafts while in the mental health facility, he may have had some appreciation for art. His antisocial behavior of fashioning items out of human body parts technically would be considered creative.

## Conscientiousness: Midrange

He worked around the community and everybody appreciated his work ethic. He seemed responsible for the most part.

## Extraversion: Low

At least for the most part. He was not outgoing or talkative, not particularly friendly (although not unfriendly), not assertive, and was not sensation-seeking most of the time.

## Agreeableness: Low

Prior to his criminal career, he was generally compliant with the rules, but he was not straightforward, altruistic, or empathic.

## Neuroticism: High

He appeared to be somewhat depressed and anxious and he had difficulty resisting temptation.

As indicated in his background, it was determined he had schizophrenia, which would explain his delusions, hallucinations, and the inappropriate laughter. Schizophrenia is a serious mental disorder that involves psychosis, a break from reality. There are five symptom criteria for this disorder. Two or more of the symptom criteria must be met in order for a person to be diagnosed with schizophrenia. At least one of the two symptoms must be delusions, hallucinations, or disorganized speech. Here are the five symptom criteria:

1. Delusions (a fixed false belief that the individual holds to be true even though presented with evidence to the contrary)

2. Hallucinations (perceiving something that does not exist, for example, hearing voices or seeing shadowy figures that are not real)

3. Disorganized speech (for example, incoherent speech, repeating words back to another person who originally said them, or rapidly moving from one topic to another)

4. Grossly disorganized or catatonic behavior

5. Negative symptoms like diminished emotional expression or avolition

In addition to schizophrenia, it would be reasonable to believe Gein had a number of paraphilias, like fetishism, necrophilia, and transvestism.

Ed Gein is quite unusual among serial killers in that there appears to be a sexual component to his crimes, but that component does not appear to be related to domination, revenge, or control, but rather a desire to re-create his mother or become his mother.

Why did Ed become a serial killer? It was probably due to a combination of factors:

- Gein did not have any meaningful relationships with women other than his mother and that relationship was highly dysfunctional. She manipulated him completely and shaped his delusional beliefs.

- He fantasized about being a woman and he was amazed by the power that he believed they had over men.

- He did not know how to relate to women and he felt conflicted because he was both attracted to and afraid of women, leaving him no prosocial ways to interact with women.

- He was fascinated by morbid topics like death, preserving body parts, and using them to create various items.

- His mother's death deprived him of all structure. In the mental health facility, Gein did fairly well, as it was a highly structured environment. A world without his mother had no form, structure, or purpose, leaving Gein lost and on a quest to find or restore meaning to his life.

- His mother regulated his behavior his entire life and without her, he had no way to manage his mood. She made him dependent on her, so dependent that her death was inconceivable to him.

- Under this intolerable stress, he connected the fact that he missed his mother with his morbid beliefs, which gave rise to this delusion where he could transform into her.

Ed Gein's delusion, this idea that he could make a suit and become his mom, is really quite unusual. Delusions that are related to schizophrenia or other disorders tied to psychosis, like delusional disorder, usually fit into a subtype, for example: grandiose, erotomanic, religious, persecutory, or jealous. Gein's delusions do not seem to fit well into any of those categories. As a matter-of-fact, what he believed does not fit into any category at all.

The closest category of delusions that are tied to Gein's beliefs would be a rare type called a delusion of misidentification. Even this type does not match too well but it may help understand this phenomenon. This type of delusion involves an incorrect belief about the identity of other people, oneself, animals, objects, or places. They all have two common elements:

- a misidentified entity
- an incorrect belief about the identity of that entity

Simply misidentifying somebody else is not normally thought of as enough to qualify as delusional.

Here are three well-known subtypes of this delusion:

1. Mirrored-self misidentification: somebody with this delusion would look in the mirror and fail to recognize their reflection. They may think the person in the mirror is someone else or they may not recognize them.

2. Fregoli delusion: This is when somebody believes that a person who they do not know (a stranger), is in fact a known person wearing a disguise.

3. Capgras delusion: This is when somebody misidentifies other people. Typically, a person with this delusion misidentifies people who are

close to them, for example, a spouse believing that their spouse has been taken over by an imposter. In most cases, multiple people are thought to be imposters, but somebody can have this delusion where there is only one misidentification.

None of these really line up with what Gein believed, but there are two lesser-known delusions of misidentification that conceptually seem closer to Gein's experience.

1. Intermetamorphosis: A belief that an individual has been transformed internally and externally to another person, so the original person no longer exists. There is also a reverse intermetamorphosis: The person believes they have transformed into somebody else.

2. Reduplicative paramnesia: This is a belief that a person, place, or object has been duplicated. With this delusion, there is no sense that the duplicate is an imposter, rather there is simply a copy of a person roaming around and interacting with various people, working, and living life. It is not unusual that people who are delusional also believe that places and objects have been duplicated.

Considering the properties of inter-metamorphosis and reduplicative paramnesia, a theory for Gein's belief structure can be put forth. Perhaps Gein had something similar to a reduplicative paramnesia, where he believed that other women who looked like his mother were sort of like duplicates. Not exact duplicates, but they were close enough to where he could essentially invest in another delusion like intermetamorphosis, which led him to believe he could transform into somebody else. Ed Gein may have put everything together to develop his morbid plan, eventually choosing to follow through with his homicidal rampage in an effort to become his mother.

## Conclusion

Ed Gein's odd behavior and the movie adaptations of it would highlight the relationship that serial killers have with their mothers and other women throughout their formative years as well as during the time they were active as a killer. His motivation is often thought to have derived from a mix of psychosis and sexual domination, with the psychosis component contributing to the particularly odd elements of his behavior, like fashioning objects out of body parts, and the sexual domination driving the homicidal part. In the next section, we will examine a motivation that appears to be more grounded in sexual domination, with a minimal or nonexistent influence from hallucinations or delusions.

# SECTION 3

## CHAPTER 6

# The Mind of the Sexual Domination Serial Killer

In this chapter, we will transition to studying the most common type of serial killer: sexual domination serial killers. These killers seem to defy our understanding of criminality. Their actions are extreme, rarely have any significant financial benefit, and often continue to escalate as the killer becomes more disorganized and careless.

This book focuses on male serial killers and female victims, but it is worth noting that there have been many exceptions to this common occurrence in the history of serial killers, including Carl Panzram, Jeffrey Dahmer, and John Wayne Gacy, all of whom raped and killed males. In some situations, serial killers have killed males to get access to females or to enhance their sense of domination over the woman, for example, James DeAngelo and Richard Ramirez.

## Relationships with Women

The foundation of most serial killers is rooted in a maladaptive view of relationships with women. This negative and dysfunctional orientation toward women usually forms in the killer's childhood, most often due to a destructive relationship with his mother. We see numerous examples of this including Ed Kemper, Carl Panzram, Richard Kuklinski, and Richard Ramirez.

## Mothers

There are many ways in which the mothers of various killers have been unusual and derelict. Some mothers have been too dominant, controlling the son and her husband, and never letting them have an opportunity to express themselves. These mothers may use strict religious beliefs as a framework for their abuse, for example, telling their sons that all sexuality is evil and demanding that their sons deny their own sexual desires. On the other hand, a mother may be too liberal, including exposing their naked body to their son, causing confusion and crossing boundaries. There have been examples of others being too distant. They did not provide any supervision to their sons or appear to have an interest in anything their sons did, including getting in trouble with the law. These abnormal mother profiles do not reliably lead to a son becoming a serial killer; rather, they simply represent another risk factor, disproportionately uncommon when examining the early history of serial killers.

## Girlfriend/Wife

The next group of serial killer/woman relationships that appear to contribute to the development of antisocial behavior toward women, would be the girlfriend or wife. A common pattern observable in several serial killers is an early failed relationship with a girlfriend/wife, for example Danny Rolling and Ted Bundy. With these two serial killers, the physical profile of the woman involved in that relationship failure, became the profile the killer would target. Danny Rolling specifically, was very particular about his targets, seeking only women that looked quite similar to his wife and stalking them for days before attacking. In certain scenarios we see that the killer was not able to establish even one meaningful relationship with a woman, for example, Joel Rifkin.

## Revenge

Difficulties with mother and girlfriend figures get combined with other factors to lead to the killer getting his revenge on various women. The women who are targeted may be known to the killer, but most often they are strangers. In a disproportionate number of cases, the women who are targeted are prostitutes, for example, Arthur Shawcross, Joel Rifkin, and Gary Ridgway.

Some have argued that this is another key relationship with women that goes wrong and contributes to the man becoming a killer in the first place, but it is more likely that the man is already configured as a killer when he first starts targeting prostitutes. Prostitutes are selected as targets because of a number of factors with their chosen career that are favorable to the killer:

- Due to the illegal nature of prostitution, there is a decreased chance that somebody will report a prostitute missing or quickly report her missing, which minimizes the risk to the serial killer of being arrested.

- Some serial killers need to justify to themselves that what they are doing is somehow right, good, or necessary. These killers have an easier time rationalizing the murder of a prostitute, who is engaging in what is typically considered a socially undesirable behavior, than they would have murdering a married mother of two who is employed as a nurse, for example.

- Prostitutes spend a lot of time with aggressive and dangerous men, who have criminal histories involving a multitude of felonies. When a prostitute is murdered, this provides the police a large number of qualified suspects, misdirecting their attention away from the actual killer.

- Serial killers are not discouraged by the fact that prostitutes charge for their services, as a murder victim will not be able to collect her fee. Gary Ridgway noted this reality all too well, saying that he could offer a prostitute any amount of money because he was not going to pay it anyway.

- From the perspective of a serial killer, prostitutes are easy to observe, which allows a serial killer to determine their routines and reduce the risk of any surprises when they are ready to commit murder.

- Some killers took advantage of word-of-mouth advertising to maintain a look of innocence, even while actively killing prostitutes. They did this by *going out* with certain prostitutes and not killing them. Knowing that these women would tell their coworkers that the killer was a nice guy and not someone to worry about, because they went out with him several times. In this way, the killers were hiding in plain sight, appearing to be just as appalled by the activity of the killer as anyone else in that group.

Most serial killers, of course, target women who are not prostitutes. They may choose their targets by seeing a woman on the street and following her to her residence or place of employment. Some killers, like James DeAngelo, Richard Ramirez, and Danny Rolling, would stalk women and then forcibly enter their homes intent on raping and killing them. One of the most frightening aspects of serial killers is the varied methods used to select victims, which makes it difficult for any potential victim to guarantee their own safety.

## Desire to Make Women Suffer

Serial killers are driven by a sadistic desire to make women suffer. The suffering of women brings the serial killer sexual pleasure and a sense of satisfaction. Some killers express their sadism purely through the act of sexual intercourse and murder, but others require even more torture to feel like they have accomplished their twisted goals. Consensual sex is often readily available to serial killers, but their seemingly insatiable desire to dominate and torture motivates them to commit sexual assault.

Some serial killers probably think of themselves more as serial rapists, who have to kill to cover their tracks, but others would kill their victims even if there was no probability of being arrested or discovered if they did not. This desire for sexual domination is not static through the killer's criminal career.

## Imaginary Relationships with Women

Serial killers think of themselves as entering into a relationship with the woman they are going to murder. The killers are setting their own standards for that relationship. It is one where they dominate physically, sexually, and emotionally. In the end, the killer takes everything from the victim in their misguided and horrible attempt to bind themselves to the victim forever.

## Collecting Women

Serial killers often believe they collect women, sometimes even believing that the women will be available to them in the afterlife. They think a special and permanent relationship has been formed. One which not even prison or death can violate or destroy. Each homicide is immutably transcribed into their book of memories. It is a short movie added to their dark and disturbing collection, available to them whenever they desire to return to the crime and recapture the feelings they had when they were perpetrating it.

Unfortunately, there are many men in the world who are dangerous, dominating, lacking in relational skill and sadistic. Why don't all these men become serial killers? The reason is because a serial killer is formed when just about everything that can go wrong does go wrong. It is in a sense a perfect storm of personality traits and environmental stressors. In addition to the inability to relate to women romantically or in any way, there are other *broken components* that occur with the quintessential serial killer. Here, I will review several of these components:

## FANTASY

This increased tendency to engage in fantasy usually develops in an early stage of the development of a serial killer. Everyone fantasizes in their life and it is usually quite healthy. People fantasize about activities like growing into an adult, going to college, starting a career, getting married, buying a car, and enjoying vacations.

Serial killers fantasize about dominating women sexually, with these fantasies occurring at surprisingly young ages. Sometimes, the object of the fantasy is the killer's mother, which ties back to what I reviewed earlier. Most people can compartmentalize their fantasies, enjoying them while simultaneously realizing that the fantasies can never actually happen. This line between fantasy and reality gets blurred with serial killers, as they minimize their chances of being arrested or being punished and start to pour fuel on the fire of their fantasy.

## SEXUAL DYSFUNCTION

In addition to the maladaptive development of romantic social abilities, serial killers often have some level of sexual dysfunction. In some cases, they cannot reach an orgasm through conventional sexual intercourse; rather, they are only able to obtain this through sadistic sexual homicide. In other cases, the serial killer can only achieve orgasm after the victim is dead, leading to acts of necrophilia.

## DESIRE FOR REVENGE

Most serial killers have a hatred of some or all women. Regardless of which women they perceive as evil, destructive, or deserving of punishment, the victim they select will experience the killer's rage as if that victim is the perceived offender. There are many examples of the ferocity driven by a desire for retribution, for example, strangulation, sodomy, beating, stabbing, mutilation, and dismemberment. The rage of the killer is so focused on the victim, that initially, many in law enforcement believe that the killer must have known the victim. They cannot understand how somebody could have so much hatred toward a stranger. Serial killers can attack a stranger with the same rage that a normal killer would have for a victim they have known and hated for many years.

## LACK OF EMPATHY

Serial killers may have the cognitive ability to understand how another person feels. This is referred to as *cognitive empathy,* and for many psychopaths, this type of empathy is intact. The type of empathy that these killers do not have is referred to as *affective empathy.* They cannot feel how others feel. When they are murdering a victim, nothing that victim says or does can invoke actual feelings in the killer.

## ESCALATION

Serial killers typically escalate in their level of dangerousness as they try to achieve, maintain or increase their level of pleasure. This escalation pattern is visible among many serial killers including James DeAngelo, Ted Bundy, and Richard Ramirez.

## Conclusion

Sexual domination killers are rare because the factors that contribute to their formation do not usually align in any given case. Even when the factors are present, the most common outcomes would not be the development of a killer. The exact mixture of genetics and environmental factors needed to form a killer is not known; however, it would be wise if society would actively try to reduce situations whereby men develop hostile attitudes toward women. If this factor were mitigated, the other factors would not likely be sufficient to facilitate the development of serial killers.

In the following chapters, I will explore the histories, crimes, and personalities of several famous serial killers. Each chapter will cover one serial killer and highlight the combination of personality traits that contributed to specific outcomes for that particular killer, for example, a killer being prolific, disorganized, emotional, cold and distant, evading arrest, committing rape and murder, engaging in sex with corpses (necrophilia), making mistakes that led to his capture.

# CHAPTER 7

# Dennis Rader: BTK

## High Openness to Experience, High Conscientiousness

Dennis Rader was a serial killer who operated in and around Wichita, Kansas from 1974 to 1991. He murdered 10 people on seven different dates, starting when he was 28 years old. He would become known as BTK, which stands for Bind Torture Kill. Rader regularly taunted authorities, which eventually led to his arrest and conviction.

## Background of Dennis Rader

Dennis Rader was born in March 1945 in Pittsburgh, Kansas. He was raised in Wichita, Kansas, the oldest of four sons. He and his brothers were often left home unsupervised. Like many serial killers, when he was young, he tortured and killed small animals. He had a particular interest in spying on female neighbors and would often steal women's undergarments and other clothing. It is believed that he had a good deal of resentment for his mother. Early in his childhood, the foundation for the development of a sexual domination killer was already visible in his poor relationship with his mother and voyeurism.

Outside of this, Rader did not have a childhood that should be considered abnormal to an outside observer. At some point when he was young, he was dropped on his head, but this information would not be readily known to observers. He also would tell police after his arrest that when he was young, he was possessed by a demon that drove him to fulfill fantasies. Disturbing information, but not something that would be known simply by looking at him.

Rader graduated from high school when he was 18 and enlisted in the Air Force when he was 21. At 26 years old he would get married and eventually have two children.

## His Serial Killer Career

### 1974-1977

His career as a serial killer started in January 1974. Rader targeted four members of a family living in a single-family home. Their ages ranged from 9 to 38 years old. He asphyxiated all of them using a rope and a plastic bag. Three months later in that same year, he murdered a 21-year-old woman, this time using a knife. This appears to be the only murder he committed that did not involve asphyxiation. Rader would wait about three years before he committed another murder. In March 1977, he killed a 28-year-old woman using a rope. In December of that same year, he murdered a 25-year-old woman using a belt. He reported this homicide to the police, which is an extremely unusual move for a serial killer.

### 1985-1991

Rader would wait over seven years before striking again. He strangled a 53-year-old woman using just his hands in April 1985. In September 1986, he would strangle a 28-year-old woman, but this time he would use a nylon stocking. His last murder was in January 1991, when he strangled a 62-year-old woman with pantyhose.

### 2004

During the time that Dennis Rader was active, he sent a substantial number of communications to law enforcement and the media, taunting them with puzzles, cryptic messages, and other types of communication. These messages would contain false information mixed with some accurate information in an effort to confuse the police and interfere with the investigation. Dennis Rader selected his own serial killer name, BTK. His communications were fairly frequent until 1979 when they abruptly stopped. Law enforcement would not hear from Rader again until 2004, at which time he sent a letter to a newspaper named the *Wichita Eagle,* in which he said that he was responsible for the 1986 murder. In that same letter he sent crime scene photographs and the driver's license of the victim, establishing that he was likely the killer or had contact with the killer. Interestingly, prior to this communication, the police did not think the same serial killer who had murdered the other women was responsible for the 1986 murder.

After this message, Rader started planting bizarre symbolic objects and cryptic messages around the Wichita area. Law enforcement was trying many different tactics to identify the killer. They had DNA from some of the crime scenes that they tried to match the suspects. They figured out that one of the letters that Rader had sent to the media was photocopied at the Wichita State University (WSU) library. Rader had sent a poem that was modeled off of another poem located in a WSU textbook.

As the police tried to develop a theory about who the killer could be, they reasoned that the killer may have been a police officer because he used police lingo in his messages. Before the 2004 message from Rader, some investigators believed the killer had died or gone to prison. Other investigators believed that the killer was still alive, but they reasoned that he was not married and probably only had superficial relationships with women. Even though this was not actually the case with Rader, this is a common assumption when investigating murders that are attributed to a serial killer.

## 2005

In February 2005, Dennis Rader sent a 3 x 5 index card and a floppy disk to a Wichita television station. The disc only contained one file, and that file only contained one sentence, which directed the police to read the index card. Sending the floppy disk was completely unnecessary to achieve his goal and would represent a crucial mistake on the part of Rader. Rader did not understand that a floppy disk contains metadata. The police were able to recover information from the disc that indicated the last person to use it was named Dennis. The metadata also identified computers in which the disc had been used. The computers were registered in just two places, a library and the church. The police discovered that the name of the church's congregation president was Dennis Rader.

The index card that Rader had sent read "Any communications have a # assigned from now on, encase one is lost were not found." Rader use the word "encase" instead of the words "in case." This threw the police off because "encase" was the name of software that they used in forensic computer investigations.

About a month before Rader sent the index card and the floppy disk, he left another clue in the bed of a pickup truck at a Home Depot in Wichita. Surveillance footage revealed that the person who left the clue was driving a black Jeep Cherokee. When the police followed up on Dennis Rader, they found he owned a vehicle matching that description.

The police took DNA from Rader's daughter, performed an analysis, and confirmed she was related to whoever it was that left the DNA at the crime scenes. The police had enough evidence to arrest Dennis Rader. After he was taken into custody, the police would learn that they missed a series of obvious clues that could have led to his arrest much earlier:

- Rader graduated from WSU, having earned a degree in criminal justice. This connected to two theories about him: he was familiar with law enforcement and associated with the University.

- Rader had worked with two of the victims and lived down the street from one of those victims.

- One of the puzzles he sent the police contained a message they should have investigated: "DRader" and "6220" (the number of his house).

Rader initially entered a plea of not guilty. His defense team didn't appear to make too much of an effort on his behalf. They probably could have had the trial postponed, but they did not try. They did not attempt to suppress any of the evidence against him and they did not request a change of venue. Rader pled guilty before the trial started. In August 2005 a judge sentenced Dennis Rader to 10 consecutive life terms with no possibility of parole for 175 years.

## Comparison to Other Sexual Domination Serial Killers

Dennis Rader has a lot in common with other sexual domination serial killers. He was obsessed with fantasies of sex, sadistic, mostly killed by strangling victims, and he kept items from the murder scene. A substantial amount of evidence was collected from his home after his arrest because of this habit. Rader would use these items to recreate the feeling that he had when he murdered his victims.

He believed that he should have received credit from the court for this behavior, as it gave him enough satisfaction as to where he did not have to kill as often. This is evidence of narcissism and potentially a separation from reality. It is hard to imagine that any serial killer would actually believe that a court might give them credit for not killing as much as they could have.

Between the homicides, Dennis Rader appeared to be a pillar of the community. He was married, had two children, maintained steady employment, was active in his church community, and served in the Air Force when he was younger.

## Personality Disorders, Including OCPD

Rader was diagnosed with three personality disorders: antisocial personality disorder and narcissistic personality disorder from cluster B, and obsessive-compulsive personality disorder (OCPD) from cluster C. In chapter 2, I discussed antisocial and narcissistic personality disorders. Here I will discuss OCPD.

### OCPD

It's fairly easy to recognize why a mental health professional would believe that Dennis Rader had antisocial and narcissistic characteristics, but what would lead them to believe that he had OCPD?

Rader worked as a city compliance officer for some time. His job was to enforce city codes and regulations, like dog leash laws and public nuisance violations. During his time in that job, he had received several complaints for bullying and being overzealous. One woman reported that she was so upset with his persistent aggressive behavior that she moved out of the area. Here we see that Rader was perfectionistic, inflexible, and stubborn.

Let's look at the definition for OCPD. This disorder is characterized by perfectionism, rigidity, negative affectivity, interpersonal aggression, as well as the need to control other people. There are eight symptom criteria listed for this disorder in the DSM, four (or more) of eight required for diagnosis:

1. Is preoccupied with details, rules, lists, order, organization, or schedules to the extent that the major point of the activities lost.

2. Shows perfectionism that interferes with task completion (e.g. is unable to complete a project because his or her own overly strict standards are not met).

3. Is excessively devoted to work and productivity to the exclusion of leisure activities and friendships (not accounted for by obvious economic necessity).

4. Is overconscientious, scrupulous, and inflexible about matters of morality, ethics, or values (not accounted for by cultural or religious identification).

5. Is unable to discard worn-out or worthless objects even when they have no sentimental value.

6. Is reluctant to delegate tasks or to work with others unless they submit to exactly his or her way of doing things.

7. Adopts a miserly spending style toward both self and others; money is viewed as something to be hoarded for future catastrophes.

8. Shows rigidity and stubbornness.

It is not clear which symptoms were recorded as endorsed by the mental health professional who made the diagnosis. When examining this list and comparing it to the information publicly available, four symptoms appear as though they may align with Rader's behavior: preoccupation with rules, perfectionism, over conscientiousness, and rigidity, but it is not possible to be sure from an outside vantage point.

When contemplating a potential personality profile for Dennis Rader, his openness to experience and conscientiousness are notable.

The Personality Characteristics of Dennis Rader

| FFM Personality Profile for Dennis Rader | | | |
|---|---|---|---|
| | HIGH | MID | LOW |
| Openness to experience | ✔ | | |
| Conscientiousness | ✔ | | |
| Extraversion | | ✔ | |
| Agreeableness | | ✔ | ✔ |
| Neuroticism | | | ✔ |

## Openness to Experience: High

Extensive investment in fantasy

## Conscientiousness: High

Good work ethic, orderly

## Extraversion: Midrange

Assertive, sensation seeking, not overly social, but did not avoid social situations

## Agreeableness: Midrange to Low

Antagonistic to the public when working as a city compliance officer

## Neuroticism: Low

Calm even in moments of high stress, although difficulty regulating anger and trouble resisting temptation

## Conclusion

Dennis Rader may have shared characteristics with other killers, but in certain areas he deviated from expectations. Rader did not have a history of trauma, which is unusual. He let a long period of time lapse between some of his murders, which is similar to James DeAngelo. Rader indicated that demons were pushing him toward homicide, which establishes a parallel with Richard Ramirez and David Berkowitz. When not successful about killing a particular victim, Rader would get upset, like Gary Ridgway. He committed the first murders after he was fired, which indicates he may have had ample time to dwell on his fantasies and have them build up in his mind.

Even with all the similarities to other killers, one of the lessons to take away from the case of Dennis Rader is that sometimes serial killers break from expected behavior and this can make them difficult to apprehend. Fortunately, Dennis Rader also made several mistakes despite his high conscientiousness, some of which the police were able to capitalize on in order to bring them to justice.

# CHAPTER 8

# Richard Ramirez: The Night Stalker

## Low Conscientiousness—Low Agreeableness

Richard Ramirez was a serial killer who was active in California from June of 1984 until August of 1985. He was convicted of 13 murders and it is believed he was responsible for several more. Ramirez was known as the Night Stalker, a name he would actually become proud of and promote during his crimes. In addition to the Night Stalker, he was also referred to as the Walk-In Killer and the Valley Intruder.

## Background of Richard Ramirez

Ramirez was born on February 29, 1960, the rarest birthday a person can have, *leap day,* which is an ironic circumstance for somebody who did not substantially fit into any known category of serial killer at the time. He was the youngest of five children. It was believed that his mother may have been exposed to toxic chemicals when she was pregnant. Like many serial killers, Ramirez had a number of head injuries as a child. In 1962, a dresser fell on his head knocking him unconscious for 15 minutes and requiring 30 stitches. He would be hit in the head with a swing in 1965, again being knocked unconscious. He started having seizures in 1966 and was diagnosed with temporal lobe epilepsy. During the same year, he saw his father physically assault his older brother.

Ramirez was first described as a loner in 1969, a frequent label we see associated with serial killers. This term connects with the theory that Ramirez may have had schizoid personality, which I will review in the mental health section.

Ramirez started using marijuana at some time near the age of 10. Around the same time, he started sleeping in the cemetery to escape his father's uncontrolled anger. In 1972, he started spending time with his older cousin, Mike, which would probably have a significant influence on Ramirez. Mike was a Vietnam War veteran who showed Ramirez photographs of women who he had sexually assaulted during the Vietnam War. Ramirez was sexually aroused by these photographs and started having fantasies about them. Near the same age, Ramirez threw a rock through a neighbor's window and his mother did nothing about it. Her indifference was almost certainly noted by Ramirez, and likely sent a fairly clear message to Ramirez that he could do whatever he wanted.

In May 1973, with Ramirez present, Mike became involved in a domestic altercation with his wife Jesse and murdered her by shooting her in the face with a .38 caliber revolver. Mike was tried for the murder, but was found not guilty by reason of insanity and was released from the Texas state mental hospital in 1977, after which he continued to exert influence on Ramirez. Also in 1973, his brother Ruben taught him how to open windows from the outside, pick locks, and disabled alarm systems. Ramirez moved in with his older sister, Ruth, and started spending time with her husband. Roberto. Roberto was a voyeur who would have Ramirez accompany him as he went out and spied on people.

From 1973 to 1977, we see a number of unusual behaviors from Ramirez. He started committing burglaries on a regular basis. LSD became a substantial part of his life and his substance use increased by him adding cocaine and heroin to the list of drugs he consumed regularly. His interest in rape and forced bondage increased, his fantasies on that topic intensify, and he started regularly having sex with prostitutes. Not long after Ramirez started working at a local hotel at age 15, he entered a woman's room and attempted to rape her, but her husband entered and severely beat Ramirez. The couple was from out-of-town and refused to come back to testify, missing a massive opportunity to stop Ramirez before he became a killer. Ramirez was sent to a juvenile detention camp.

The antisocial behavior of Ramirez continued over the next several years. After being released from custody he skipped school, his grades plummeted, and he dropped out of high school at age 17. Mike and Ramirez resumed spending time together in 1977 after Mike's release from a mental hospital. Ramirez developed significant tooth decay from his substance use and from consuming a great deal of candy, indicating his lack of ability to resist temptation. By age 18, he was worshiping Satan and believed that Satan protected him

From 1978 through 1984, Ramirez was arrested several times for auto theft, stealing other items, burglary, and possession. He gave up on any attempts at maintaining personal hygiene. Not long after this we see he began his career as a serial killer.

## The Crimes of Richard Ramirez

Ramirez was 24 years old when he started committing homicide.

**1984**

On April 10, 1984, a nine-year-old female was murdered in the basement of the hotel where Ramirez was living. It was not until 2009 that his DNA was matched to a sample obtained from the crime scene but he was never charged with this crime.

The body of a 79-year-old woman was found in her apartment in Glassell Park, California on June 28, 1984. She had been stabbed repeatedly as she slept and her body was almost decapitated. A fingerprint found on a mesh screen connected Ramirez to this crime.

**1985**

The rest of the murders committed by Ramirez occurred in 1985. On March 17, Ramirez committed crimes in two different locations. The first one was when Ramirez attacked a 22-year-old woman outside of her house in Rosemead, California and shot her with a .22 caliber pistol. This victim would survive. Ramirez then went into her house and shot her 34-year-old roommate once in the head, killing her. The second crime occurred not long after this in Monterey Park, California. Ramirez pulled a 30-year-old woman out of her car and shot her twice. She did not survive.

Ramirez made entry into a house of a married couple in Whittier, California. He shot a 64-year-old man while he was sleeping, then bound and raped the victim's 44-year-old wife. After the rape, Ramirez started stealing valuables from the house and the woman managed to free herself and retrieve a shotgun. She pointed the shotgun at Ramirez but it was not loaded. He shot her three times with the .22 caliber pistol before retrieving a knife and stabbing her.

Ramirez made entry into another home in Monterey Park on May 14. The occupants were a 66-year-old husband and his 63-year-old disabled wife. The husband tried to retrieve his own firearm after seeing Ramirez come into his bedroom, but Ramirez shot him in the face with a .22 caliber pistol. Ramirez then raped his wife and stole valuables from the home. The wife survived, but the husband died later at the hospital.

Ramirez drove a stolen car to the site of his next murder. On May 29 he broke into a house in Monrovia, California, which was occupied by two sisters, one who was 83 years old and another who was 81 years old. He attacked them with a hammer, tortured the 83-year-old with electricity, and raped the 81-year-old. Before he left, he used her lipstick to draw a pentagram on her thigh and on the walls of two bedrooms. It was two days before they were found. The 83-year-old would later die.

Ramirez's next crime was on May 30 in Burbank, California, where he made his way into the home of a 42-year-old mother and her 11-year-old son, handcuffing both of them. Ramirez made the boy lead him to where valuable property was kept so he could steal it and then he repeatedly raped the mother.

Ramirez targeted a house at random in Arcadia, California on July 2, 1985. The occupant was a 75-year-old woman. As she was sleeping, Ramirez attacked her with a lamp until she was unconscious and then stabbed her with a knife he found in the kitchen. She did not survive.

On July 5, 1985, Ramirez would target a house in Sierra Madre, California, where he found a 16-year-old female resident asleep in her bedroom. He bludgeoned her with a tire iron before searching for a knife in the kitchen. When he was unable to find a knife, he started to strangle her with a telephone cord, but when he saw sparks coming from the cord, he believed that Jesus had intervened to save this victim and he fled the scene. Although she required 478 stitches on her head, she survived the attack.

July 7, on this day we see two separate crime scenes, Ramirez makes entry into a house with a 61-year-old female occupant, he beat her to death using his fists and by kicking her, he left a sneaker print on her face. Not long after this he targeted the house of a 63-year-old woman, he handcuffed her, attempted to rape her, and demanded that she "swear to Satan" when she told him that he had taken everything of value.

Ramirez would produce two crime scenes on July 20 as well. The first one was in Glendale, California, where he made entry into a house while carrying a machete that he had acquired beforehand. He then attacked a 68-year-old man and his 66-year-old wife with the machete before eventually shooting them with a .22 caliber pistol. Before stealing their valuables, he mutilated their bodies. The second crime scene was a house in Sun Valley, California. There he targeted a 32-year-old man, a 29-year-old woman, and their eight-year-old son. He killed the man with a .25 caliber pistol and then raped the woman and her son. The couple's two-year-old daughter was also in that house, but was not harmed. Ramirez demanded that the couple "swear to Satan" that they were not hiding money from him, before stealing their valuables and fleeing the scene.

Ramirez's next attack would occur in Northridge, California on August 6, when he broke into the home of a 38-year-old man and a 27-year-old woman, shooting both of them with a. 25 caliber pistol. The man, who was shot in the neck, managed to fight off Ramirez and avoid two more shots that Ramirez fired. Ramirez managed to escape and both victims survived.

The next target for Ramirez was a couple in Diamond Bar, California on August 8. The husband, who was 35 years old, was shot and killed by Ramirez. Ramirez then raped the victim's 28-year-old wife. The familiar demand of asking the victims to "swear to Satan" was repeated in this crime except here Ramirez wanted assurances the victim would not scream during the rape. When the woman's three-year-old son entered the bedroom during the rape, Ramirez tied him up before continuing sexual assault.

During this rampage of rape, murder, and theft, Ramirez had been paying attention to the media coverage and realized that the search for him was intensifying. He drove from Los Angeles to the San Francisco Bay Area and targeted a home there on August 18. He shot a 66-year-old man in the head with a .25 caliber pistol and then raped and beat his 62-year-old wife. He then shot her in the head as well. Before leaving he drew a pentagram and the phrase "Jack the Knife" on the bedroom wall using lipstick.

Ramirez targeted a house in Mission Viejo, California on August 24. A 13-year-old boy in the house heard Ramirez walking outside and woke his parents. The father raced outside thinking that he was chasing away a burglar. The police were able to locate a footprint from Ramirez and they were given a description of his car by the father.

Shortly after this on the same date, Ramirez climbed through an open window into a house with a 29-year-old man and 27-year-old woman. He shot the male three times in the head then informed the woman that he was the Night Stalker, before repeatedly raping her. Ramirez made two references to Satan during this attack. He punched the victim as he demanded she swear she loved Satan and made her "swear to Satan" that there were no more valuables in the house he had not located. The woman was able to make it to the window to see what type of vehicle Ramirez was driving, which is information she provided to the police later. Both of these victims survived.

## Capture

Police managed to identify Richard Ramirez as the suspect based on a fingerprint found on one of the stolen vehicles used, signaling the beginning of the end of his homicidal rampage.

On August 30, Ramirez traveled by bus to Arizona to meet his brother, returning to Los Angeles on August 31. At this point he became aware that he had been identified as it was widely reported in the media. He ran across the highway and attempted to carjack three separate vehicles, but eventually a mob chased him down and beat him until the police arrived.

## Conviction, Sentence and Death

His trial started on July 22, 1988. On August 14 one of the jurors in the case was murdered, creating concern that the murder might have been arranged by Ramirez, but as it turns out, the juror was murdered by her boyfriend who later committed suicide.

On September 20, 1989, Ramirez was convicted of 43 different crimes, including 13 counts of murder and sentenced to death on November 7, 1990.

Ramirez would die at age 53 on June 7, 2013 from B-cell lymphoma complicated by substance abuse and Hepatitis C.

## Mental Health and Personality

### ANTISOCIAL PERSONALITY DISORDER

Many have made the argument that the behavior of Ramirez aligns with antisocial personality disorder, although it is not clear if he ever received a mental health diagnosis to this effect. When looking at the symptoms associated with this disorder, it is easy to see why some believe there is a match here: repeated crimes, lying, impulsivity, aggressiveness, reckless disregard for safety, irresponsibility, and lack of remorse.

### PSYCHOPATHY

Whether Ramirez had antisocial personality disorder or not, his behavior does seem to have a relationship with Factor 2 (secondary) psychopathy. Ramirez demonstrated criminal versatility through an incredible variety of criminal acts including stealing vehicles, selling drugs, homicide, rape, assault, burglary, theft. He appeared to be excitement seeking, did not have long term goals, was a juvenile delinquent, and was impulsive and irresponsible.

There is also potential overlap with Factor 1 (primary) psychopathy as indicated by his lack of remorse, shallow affect, lack of empathy, failure to accept responsibility, pathological lying, and grandiosity. Ramirez did not appear to have too much in a way of superficial charm or manipulation ability, as both of those convey the ability to be insidious. Ramirez was blunt and straightforward in his criminal acts, not employing the use of any degree of finesse or subtlety. Not surprisingly, Richard could also be considered narcissistic, which was clearer after his arrest when there were opportunities for him to attempt to impress his group of fans.

### SCHIZOID PERSONALITY DISORDER

Considering that Ramirez was so aggressive, it seems odd that schizoid personality disorder has been brought up in reference to his case; however, a mental health clinician who assessed Ramirez believed that he may have had this disorder. Schizoid personality disorder is a cluster A personality disorder (odd, eccentric). Its symptoms include being uninterested in close relationships, choosing to be alone, having little interest in sex with another person, not taking pleasure in activities, not having close friends, appearing indifferent to praise or criticism, and being cold and detached. There appear to be some schizoid features that align with his behavior, but it is not clear if his behavior would qualify him for the disorder.

### PSYCHOTIC

There is also a theory that Ramirez was psychotic. This theory is supported by his belief that Satan was protecting him as Ramirez committed homicide, which is consistent with a mystical delusion. It is possible he had something like delusional disorder or some other disorder associated with hallucinations and delusions, although there is no way to know for certain. He used substances so heavily for so long, the use could have caused cognitive processing difficulties that could be mistaken for psychosis. His level of impulsivity was also exceedingly high, which could be confused with psychotic thinking.

Let us take a look at his potential personality profile:

| FFM Personality Profile for Richard Ramirez | | | |
|---|:---:|:---:|:---:|
| | HIGH | MID | LOW |
| Openness to experience | ✔ | | |
| Conscientiousness | | | ✔ |
| Extraversion | | | ✔ |
| Agreeableness | | | ✔ |
| Neuroticism | | ✔ | |

## Openness to Experience: High

He was adventurous, experienced emotions intensely, and had a high investment in fantasies, which were destructive in nature but technically would still count.

## Conscientiousness: Extremely Low

This is perhaps the most salient personality trait for Ramirez. He was highly disorganized, impulsive, capricious, and immature.

## Extraversion: Low

Ramirez had a high degree of sensation seeking, but had low extraversion in most every other way. He was not friendly or outgoing and did not have a good deal of positive emotion.

## Agreeableness: Extremely Low

Ramirez was exceedingly willing to torture, rape, and kill victims at a moment's notice. He had low empathy, distrusted people, and did not look out for the greater good to any extent.

## Neuroticism: Midrange

Even though the level of neuroticism would be midrange overall for Ramirez, the facets have extreme scores in opposite directions. He was not self-conscious or vulnerable and he was calm during times of extremely high stress. At the same time, he had difficulty resisting temptation and a tremendous amount of anger.

## Analysis

### SEXUAL DOMINATION

What makes Ramirez unusual as a serial killer? Ramirez was technically a sexual domination serial killer, but he was unusual in this category because he was particularly sadistic and disorganized. More so than many other serial killers, he had contact with many victims that ultimately survived. During the time he was active he assaulted and/or raped at least 14 victims that he did not kill, even though he tried to kill many of them. Some he let live even though he had a clear opportunity to take their lives.

It was not always clear what was motivating Ramirez or what his overall strategy was. He seemed to enjoy the thrill of murder, rape, and assault without having a need to necessarily kill every victim. This is highly unusual for a sexual domination serial killer. When this type of killer fails to kill an intended victim, they consider this a disastrous error; however, it does not appear that Ramirez cared or understood the consequences of leaving potential witnesses behind. It seems fairly clear he did not let victims live out of any form of mercy or compassion, so we are left to assume he was simply that impulsive and haphazard. The judge who sentenced him to die said that his actions demonstrated cruelty, callousness, and viciousness beyond any human understanding, which seems to sum up his brutality fairly well.

### BRUTALITY AND EXPEDIENCE

Many serial killers have killed more people then Ramirez,

but few have done so in such a short period of time and with the level of brutality demonstrated by Ramirez. He terrorized several communities in 1985, and left a trail of destruction, including many people who sustained horrible physical injuries and posttraumatic stress disorder.

He did not wait for victims to come to him; rather, he was aggressive and otherwise made entry into people's houses, sometimes by breaking in, but most of the time entering through an unlocked or open window. During times when a serial killer is loose in a community, residents who are particularly worried sometimes stay at home, believing that they are increasing their chances of not becoming a victim. With Richard Ramirez, the strategy made little difference in the amount of risk. No one felt safe with Ramirez on the loose.

Ramirez took a tremendous number of chances in his criminal activities. He was not particularly careful about evidence being left behind most of the time, although he did wipe down vehicles that he had stolen to remove his fingerprints. One of those fingerprints that he missed led to his arrest.

It is a little puzzling why Ramirez would be so careless when attacking people inside homes, but would take the time to wipe fingerprints away from a car. It stands to reason that in the heat of the moment, while committing homicide and rape, he could not control himself. Pure rage consumed his every thought and behavior, but when he was in his vehicle he was able to think more clearly.

### CHOICE OF WEAPONRY AND THEFT BEHAVIORS

Another area where he diverged from other serial killers was his use of a large variety of weapons, for example: .22 caliber revolver, .25 caliber automatic, various knives, a lamp, a hammer, electrical cord, telephone cord, a machete, a tire iron, fists, and feet. He was equally as indiscriminate with his theft behaviors, stealing cash, jewelry, or any other valuable that he thought he could sell to fuel his substance use habit. Stealing property was an important part of his strategy, but his potential take from any particular crime did not seem to influence which victims he selected.

## AGE PREFERENCES

Ramirez did not appear to have any age preference for his victims, with the age ranges being more extreme than observed with many other killers. He was willing to attack people independent of their age, physical characteristics, the presence of children in the house, the existence or lack of prior relationship, and their physical location.

## HIS PACE & SURVIVAL

The pace that Ramirez maintained greatly separates him from the expected behavior of serial killers. Many serial killers will take at least a short break after homicide, perhaps a week, a month or even more. Ramirez sometimes raped and killed multiple victims on the same day, sometimes just hours apart. This behavior has a parallel to Ted Bundy. Toward the end of his criminal career, Bundy attacked four female college students in the Chi Omega sorority house in Tallahassee, Florida, killing two and seriously wounding two others, before being scared away by a sorority sister who was returning from a late date with her boyfriend. The two victims he murdered, he did so by strangulation. The other two were beaten with a club. Even after exerting all this energy in these heinous attacks, he walked several blocks away and broke into an apartment of another young woman. He attacked her and broke her jaw and caused nerve damage, before being scared by people who had heard noises and were knocking and calling on the phone. This was the only time in Bundy's criminal career where he attacked that many people in such a short period of time. Many people believed he was trying to go out in a blaze of glory, doing what he wanted to do and throwing caution to the wind. Ramirez maintained a pace similar to this over a longer period of time. In this sense, he emulated the tremendous rage and recklessness of Bundy in an amplified fashion.

The last unusual characteristic is that Ramirez actually lived through his crime spree. It was common knowledge that a serial killer was loose in that area who was sneaking in or breaking into people's homes. Gun sales increased dramatically during that time and yet no one was able to engage him with a loaded firearm during the commission of his crimes. Ramirez was beaten badly by a crowd on the day he was arrested, which could have easily led to his death, but the police saved his life.

## Conclusion

What made Ramirez into such a rage-filled killer? He was exposed to myriad negative elements when he was young, but this happens to a lot of people. What makes Ramirez different in this dimension? Is just how young he was when these factors started influencing him? For example: toxic chemicals in utero, the concussions at two and at five, using marijuana at age 10, the disturbing photographs and stories from his cousin Mike at 12, and witnessing a homicide at age 13. Was there too much environmental stress at such a young age? It is not clear if Ramirez ever had a chance at a productive life. His introduction to substances only added fuel to the fire and escalated his level of violence, as the need for drugs became another insatiable desire.

CHAPTER 9

# Gary Ridgway:
# The Green River Killer

## High Conscientiousness—Low Neuroticism

Gary Ridgway, also known as the Green River Killer, was one of the most prolific serial killers who has ever lived. It is believed he killed at least 71 people, although the actual number could be substantially more than the official count. Gary Ridgway himself lost track of how many people he had murdered. He was eventually convicted of 49 murders after one of the longest and most extensive criminal investigations in United States history.

## Gary Ridgway's Background

Ridgway was born in Salt Lake City, Utah on February 18, 1949. His family moved to King County, Washington when he was 11 years old. He had one elder and one younger brother. Ridgway's mother was dominant and aggressive and his father was submissive. She reportedly broke plates over her husband's head, which elicited no reaction from him.

Ridgway's father introduced him to the idea of necrophilia. His father had worked in a mortuary when Ridgway was young and would return from work and tell stories of a coworker who apparently engaged in sex acts with the corpses. This became one of Ridgway's fantasies as a teenager. He liked the idea of it because there were no feelings involved and it was difficult to get caught.

Ridgway was a chronic bedwetter when he was young, which deeply offended his mother. While barely dressed herself, she would scold him and give him a cold bath paying attention to what she referred to as his "dirtiest parts." She maintained terrible boundaries with Ridgway, often talking about her sexual behavior. He would eventually develop an attraction for her and fantasize about raping and killing her.

There were several other warning signs that the future was dark for Gary Ridgway. He performed poorly in school, killed animals, set fires, and had an extreme obsession with true crime. In addition to the bedwetting behavior, the other two behaviors of the MacDonald Triad were present: killing animals and setting fires. It is believed that Ridgway drowned a boy in a lake when he was young, but this report was never confirmed. Ridgway stabbed a boy in the woods one day after school. He was never arrested for this crime, but police confirmed with the victim years later that the crime did in fact happen. The boy was taken to the hospital and recovered.

Despite being held back two grades, Ridgway did eventually graduate high school in 1969; his IQ was in the low eighties. That same year he entered the Navy, and, in 1970, he married his first wife, who he had known for several years. As part of the service in the Navy, he spent some time in the Philippines, where he claims that he first had sex with prostitutes. While Ridgway was overseas, his wife started having an affair. Upon his return to King County in July of 1971, his wife requested a divorce. It is reasonable to believe that this incident contributed to Ridgway's already distorted view of women.

In August of 1971, he began working as a truck painter at a Kenworth plant, a job he would keep for 30 years until he was arrested in 2001. This is highly atypical for a serial killer. Usually they have poor work experiences involving several low-paying jobs that they only keep for a short time.

Ridgway married again in 1973 and had a son in 1975. His second wife reported that Ridgway was interested in bondage and liked having sex outdoors. She noticed that he would be out late into the evening, a behavior that he would eventually stop trying to explain. When they would walk together in the woods, he liked to hide from her and then sneak up behind her and scare her. He took pride in his ability to walk without making noise. At one point he choked her using his forearm and upper arm, which would become a tactic he would use in the future on other women with lethal consequences. The couple separated in 1980 and divorced about a year later. She took custody of their son and Ridgway contemplated killing her because he had to pay child support.

Ridgway bought a house in King County. Other than a brief time he had some renters, he lived there alone until 1985, moving only two more times before his arrest in 2001. During this period, he dated quite a bit and frequently solicited prostitutes, developing a sense of rage and disgust toward them. He was engaged to one woman, but she broke up with him after she met someone else, adding yet another perceived offense caused by a woman to Ridgway's list. In 1985, Ridgway met the woman who became his third wife. She moved in a few months later, they were married in 1988 and would remain so until 2002.

## The Crimes of Gary Ridgway

### 1982

This case starts on July 15, 1982, when the body of 16-year-old Wendy Lee Cofield was found in the Green River, in King County, Washington. From August 13 to 15, four more bodies of young women were found in or around the Green River. All the victims thus far were believed to be prostitutes. The unknown perpetrator was called the Green River Killer.

## 1983

On August 16, the Green River task force was formed, but the police would not make any progress until April 30, 1983. This is the first time the police became aware of Ridgway. The boyfriend of a missing woman, Marie Malvar, watched her get into a dark-colored pickup truck as she was soliciting on the street. He noticed the driver of the truck and Marie seemed to be in an argument, which prompted him to follow the pickup, but he lost it at a traffic light. The boyfriend never saw Marie again. Less than a week after that incident, the boyfriend was with Marie's father and brother when they spotted that same truck near where the boyfriend had lost contact with it before. They followed the truck until it arrived at a house and called the police, who arrived and spoke with the owner of the house, Gary Ridgway.

Ridgway denied ever having seen Marie Malvar, which satisfied the police who then left and never followed up. Unfortunately, the boyfriend's description of the vehicle and the driver was not detailed. Not long after, a witness described a similar truck that was used in the abduction of another prostitute and notified the police, but this information and the prior incident with the truck was never connected by the police. The police were highly focused at that time on another suspect who was a taxi driver. This suspect knew five of the victims and from the perspective of the police, looked quite promising as the killer. They eventually charged him for unpaid parking tickets.

The police actually had contact with Ridgway several times and they reported him as cooperative. Ridgway admitted soliciting and physically assaulting prostitutes. He acknowledged he had contact with the victims. He would eventually pass a polygraph, which unfortunately, many law enforcement agencies believe are accurate, even though scientific research has repeatedly established that polygraphs are pseudoscientific nonsense.

**1984**

By November 1983 the number of victims was up to 11, prompting anger about the effectiveness of the Green River task force. The task force was put under new leadership, but by December of 1984, the number of victims would reach 42. The Green River Killer appeared to be unstoppable.

The police would get a break around that same time, but they were unable to effectively take advantage of it. One victim escaped and provided valuable info to police including the fact that her attacker had a Kenworth Trucking Co ID (he showed her after she asked if he was the Green River Killer). The police confronted Ridgway, but he said the victim bit him first. The victim refused to file charges against Ridgway.

**1987**

By April 1987, with the number of victims now at 46, the police strongly suspected that Ridgway was the killer. They searched his house, his locker at work, and his vehicles, taking hundreds of items with them including ropes, carpet fibers, plastic tarps, samples of paint, and his financial records. Nothing tied Ridgway to the crimes other than the fact that he was the last person who was seen with two victims. It did not seem important at the time, but the police also collected DNA.

**1990**

By the end of 1990, the Green River task force was essentially disbanded, with only one full-time and one part-time detective still working on a case. By 1991, the task force had spent over $15,000,000.

## His Capture

In March of 2001, the Washington State crime lab started using a new method of DNA testing. By September, DNA found at crime scenes was matched to Gary Ridgway. On November 16, 2001, Ridgway was arrested for attempting to pick up an undercover officer posing as a prostitute, after which she was released. Two weeks later, on November 30, 2001, Ridgway was arrested and charged with four counts of aggravated murder in the first degree. On March 27, 2003, Ridgway was charged with three additional counts of murder. There were still 42 cases for which Ridgway was not charged as there was little or no evidence connecting Ridgway to the crimes.

## Conviction, Sentence, and Death

In June of 2003, the King County prosecutor entered into a plea agreement with Gary Ridgway. The prosecution did not seek the death penalty, but rather asked for life in prison with no possibility to appeal the conviction or the sentence. Ridgway would have to plead guilty to all the murders he committed and provide truthful information about all his crimes, including locations of all undiscovered remains of victims. In addition, he would have to answer any questions during interviews conducted by investigators. If he was found to be responsible for a crime that he failed to disclose, he could be executed.

The prosecution did not want to have 42 cases remain unsolved, even if they had a strong feeling that Ridgway was responsible. It was their belief that the families of the victims would like to see Ridgway held accountable for all the murders he committed, not just a few where there was sufficient evidence. This has been a hotly debated decision. It is worth noting that Ridgway identified several cases in which he was not a suspect, so the family members of those victims were able to have some sort of closure that they never would have without the plea agreement.

On November 5, 2003, Gary Ridgway, 54 at the time, pleaded guilty to 48 counts of aggravated first-degree murder, and in December, he was sentenced to life in prison without the possibility of parole.

In December 2010, another victim's skull was found in a

ravine in Auburn, Washington. Her name was Rebecca Marrero. She was last seen in December of 1982, but not reported missing until July of 1984. Ridgway had already confessed to her murder, but charges were not pursued because they could not find her body and they already had him on 48 counts of murder.

On February 7, 2011, Ridgway was charged with Marrero's murder and 11 days later he pleaded guilty. He is currently serving his life sentence.

Let's take a look at Gary Ridgway's potential personality profile:

### FFM Personality Profile for Gary Ridgway

| | HIGH | MID | LOW |
|---|---|---|---|
| Openness to experience | | ✔ | |
| Conscientiousness | ✔ | | |
| Extraversion | | ✔ | |
| Agreeableness | | | ✔ |
| Neuroticism | | | ✔ |

## Openness to Experience: Midrange

He really stood out as particularly creative or intellectually curious, but he was somewhat adventurous.

## Conscientiousness: High

Ridgway was extremely cautious during his criminal activity, always being cognizant of what evidence he was leaving behind. It is highly unusual for a serial killer's house to be turned upside down by the police without immediately useful evidence being collected. Ridgway was also a productive employee who was able to stay at his job for many years without incident (he was awarded for perfect attendance). I will review additional evidence pointing toward conscientiousness toward the end of this chapter.

## Extraversion: Midrange

One of the reasons Ridgway was able to get away with his crimes for so long was that to some he did appear friendly enough to not attract negative attention. He was also sensation seeking and somewhat assertive, but not particularly outgoing.

## Agreeableness: Low

Ridgway had no empathy for his victims, and was not straightforward, trusting, modest, or altruistic.

## Neuroticism: Low

He was in a number of situations where he was almost arrested by the police and yet he did not lose his composure. Even when he was arrested for soliciting an undercover police officer, he did not seem to be particularly worried. Many serial killers are extremely emotionally reactive, but Ridgway was not. He was not self-conscious, depressed, anxious, or particularly susceptible to anger outbursts (although there were notable exceptions to this facet).

## Analysis

### PRIMARY AND SECONDARY PSYCHOPATHY

Ridgway's behavior aligned with a number of primary and secondary psychopathic characteristics like grandiosity, superficial charm, and being manipulative, but one feature that really stands out was his tendency to deceive. He admitted he was a pathological liar and even had difficulty telling the truth under the threat of the death penalty. The resistance to being truthful was partially based on the fact that he knew that a popular true crime author may be writing a book on him and he wanted to appear in the best possible light. This touches not only on pathological lying but narcissism.

Ridgway's superficial charm and manipulation skills were a key reason why he was an effective killer. He was not physically large enough to dominate women in every single situation. He relied on his ability to con them into believing he was trustworthy and putting them in a vulnerable position. He would do things like lend future victims a vehicle, find them a job, give them food, show them a picture of his son, become a regular customer, and offer more money. He noted that it didn't matter how much he offered, as he was never going to lose anything because he was going to kill them.

Initially, he said none of his crimes were premeditated, but rather they were committed in a moment of rage. He said killing released pressure that accumulated from child support payments, his divorces, poor sleep, and his inability to stick up for himself. If his claims were true, his behavior would be inconsistent with low neuroticism, but as it turns out, he admitted later these claims were false.

He initially did not admit to every killing that was attributed to the Green River Killer, because he did not want to risk claiming to have killed a woman unless he actually did it. This action would violate a type of code that he maintained as a serial killer. He took pride in what he did and he did not want to take that from any other killer.

Ridgway's had an extraordinarily good recall of past events; however, his excellent memory failed when thinking about the women he murdered. He said that they didn't mean anything to him and once they were murdered, he did not keep their memory, rather he simply knew where he left the bodies.

Sometimes Ridgway would not be able to kill a selected victim, and he would be enraged because he had wasted all the time and energy in preparation. When this happened, it would increase his desire to kill. When the women would see him shaking, he would have to explain it away as anxiety.

## HIS METHODS

Ridgway's method was fairly consistent: get behind the victim and strangle her by compressing her neck in the crook of his arm and then using his other arm to add force. Some of the struggles took as long as two minutes. Sometimes, before he actually attempted to commit murder, the victims would sense it and start pleading with him to spare them. He was never moved to compassion. The selection of strangulation as a method was because it was more personal and rewarding than using a gun. Ridgway used to worry about forgetting the location of one of the bodies, because knowing where they were buried gave him a sense of ownership of the victims.

Ridgway's only regret was that he left too much evidence. He believed himself to be a victim of technology, because no detective ever caught him, it was the DNA that led to his downfall.

## HIGHLY CONSCIENTIOUS

As I mentioned earlier in this chapter, there is a good deal of evidence supporting the theory that Ridgway was highly conscientious. Here I will review a few of the things he did that indicate a high score in this trait.

His criminal activities were characterized by extremely careful planning, including selecting victims after hours of surveillance. If a potential victim was accompanied by somebody else, he would not kill the victim; rather, he would go on a date to build a stable reputation. After he selected a victim, he would flash money at them as he drove by in his car, then pull off the road into a parking lot, this was done to minimize his chances of being identified. Even though Ridgway was once arrested for soliciting an undercover police officer, he was fairly careful about the police tactic of having an officer pose as a prostitute. He would often watch other transactions to ensure that the victim was actually a prostitute and not a police officer.

On the occasions where he was scratched by a victim, he

would cut her fingernails off before disposing of the body and use battery acid to cover deep scratches on his body. He would always use gloves and be mindful not to leave behind fingerprints. One time he realized he left tire tracks driving away from a dumpsite. He replaced the tires on his truck and disposed of the originals. After he dumped the body, he would call the prostitutes pimp to arrange another date, running under the reasoning that the pimp would not expect a killer to behave in this manner.

Ridgway was fully aware that the police would scour the crime scenes and chase down every possible piece of evidence. He used to drop cigarette butts and gum at the crime scenes to throw the police off, because he did not use either one. In addition, he would leave airport motel pamphlets and car rental papers behind, so that the police would think he was a traveling businessman and not someone who lived in that local community. In February 1984, he sent a letter to the newspaper to throw off the task force. An FBI expert confidently declared that the letter was not written by the Green River Killer.

Now obviously Ridgway broke the rules of society, which is inconsistent with conscientiousness, but he followed his own rules, which he set to prevent him from being arrested. He appears to have a high level on all of the other areas of conscientiousness. A high score in this trait is what made Ridgway so dangerous. Typically, serial killers are low in conscientiousness and the impulsivity leads to a number of mistakes. Ridgway was careful and understood the consequences of being caught. He took the time to develop a strategy that reduced his risk of being caught.

### PERFECT STORM OF TRAITS
It was a perfect storm of traits. His psychopathic behaviors did not include impulsivity and irresponsibility. His behavior was narcissistic, but not in an obvious way that would attract

attention. For example, he did not attract the attention of the police when they interviewed him. He did not appear arrogant and did not deny what they already knew. He cooperated with police throughout any questioning, even agreeing to take a polygraph. Ridgway did not ask for an attorney, even though he had a right to an attorney. Ridgway was married, which is somewhat unusual for serial killers and decreased how suspicious he looked. Many people believed him to be normal; they did not detect paranoia and he had no significant substance use.

In the case of Gary Ridgway, conscientiousness only amplified the destructive potential of his psychopathy. This is what made Ridgway more dangerous than almost every other serial killer in history. Early in his criminal career, he was impulsive, but the police failed to catch him. He was able to capitalize on their failure and more efficiently express his conscientiousness.

## Conclusion

What caused Ridgway to become a serial killer? As with all killers, the etiology is complex, but Ridgway certainly had a number of factors that are associated with serial killing. He had a poor relationship with his mother. Destructive ideas were made available to him at a young age. When his first wife had an affair, it made a significant impression on him and contributed to his hatred of women. After all that, he was enraged again when another woman rejected him.

Ridgway is considered the second most prolific serial killer in United States history, behind Samuel Little. Ridgway had what one could argue was the worst possible combination of traits. These traits enabled him to kill without remorse, to get away with it, and left him with an insatiable desire to continue committing serial homicides.

CHAPTER 10

# Joel Rifkin

## High Openness to Experience, Low Extraversion

Joel Rifkin was a serial killer who was active in New York City for four years starting in 1989. Even though he was convicted for the murders of nine victims, it is believed he may have killed up to 17 women. He appeared to have extremely high openness to experience, as indicated by a substantial investment in fantasies, and extremely low extraversion, which was most evident in his tendency to remain isolated and form few relationships.

## Background of Joel Rifkin

Rifkin was born in New York City on January 20, 1959, and was adopted three weeks later by Ben and Jeannie Rifkin. His family moved to East Meadow on Long Island when he was six years old. Growing up, he had numerous problems in school and was frequently targeted by bullies. They called him the turtle because of how he was naturally hunched over and due to his slow, unsteady gait. Dyslexia caused his grades to suffer. There are reports that claim he had an IQ of 128, which is almost two standard deviations above the mean, and places Rifkin above the 97th percentile, meaning his IQ score was greater than or equal to 97% of the population.

Rifkin's struggle with bullies went on for many years and became extreme. He was uncoordinated, accident-prone, and not good at athletic endeavors, which supplied his classmates with a pretense for continuous attacks. In high school the bullying escalated, including more physical violence like striking him with eggs, submerging his head in the toilet, and pulling his pants down. His academic performance declined even more due to the bullying because he began actively avoiding other students, would be late to class, and would be the last to leave so that he was left alone.

Rifkin would spend his time alone in his room and eventually started fantasizing about sex. Many of these fantasies also included violence, a familiar theme when looking at serial killers. One fantasy included women fighting each other to be with him in some type of gladiatorial combat. Sometimes these imaginary fights were to the death.

Rifkin took an interest in photography and his parents even bought him a new camera. He joined the high school yearbook committee, but no sooner did he join, when some of his classmates stole his camera. Despite the adversity, he decided to stay on the committee working on non-photography related items. The committee successfully completed the yearbook and held a party to celebrate; however, they did not invite Rifkin. This particularly cruel and overt rejection had a profound impact on him, contributing to his return to spending time alone in his bedroom. It was at this time that he started taking an interest in books about serial killers. He also developed a keen interest in the 1972 movie named *Frenzy*, an Alfred Hitchcock film about a serial killer. The scenes in the movie where female victims were strangled were particularly exciting for him.

After graduating high school in 1977, Rifkin attended college, but he was unable to make friends and he remained isolated. He dropped out, enrolled at another college, and dropped out again. Rifkin started dating prostitutes around the time he graduated from high school, even though he had extreme difficulty talking to women. In his relationships with prostitutes, he did not run into the same difficulty, perhaps due to the nature of the relationship as a provider and a client as opposed to two people that may be romantically involved under circumstances that do not involve a financial transaction. His frequent sex with prostitutes started to become like an addiction. Rifkin kept soliciting prostitutes to the point where it had a significant financial effect on him. He would use any money that he had for prostitutes and started to neglect work and college.

In February of 1987, when Rifkin was 28, his father Ben was diagnosed with cancer and committed suicide. Seven months later, Rifkin was arrested for soliciting an undercover police officer. In March 1989, Rifkin committed his first murder, which I will talk about more in the next section. Not long after this he started a landscaping company, which failed in 1991, leading to Rifkin working a series of part-time jobs.

## Joel Rifkin Homicides

### 1989

In March of 1989, 30-year-old Joel Rifkin, drove from his family's home in Long Island, New York to New York City after his mother and sister left the home on vacation. After arriving, he picked up a prostitute and brought her back home. While there, she slept and used heroin. Eventually Rifkin became aggravated and struck her in the head with a shell casing from a howitzer, then strangled her. He removed her fingerprints and teeth and cut her body up into six parts, which he dumped in areas throughout New Jersey and New York. On March 5, the victim's head was discovered on a golf course in New Jersey, but she would not be identified until 2013. When Rifkin heard the news that the victim was discovered, he became extremely afraid of being arrested, which led to him promising himself that he would never kill again.

### 1991-1993

Breaking his promise, Rifkin resumed killing in 1991. From 1991 through 1993, he committed a series of murders. All of the victims were believed to be prostitutes. There is debate about when the murders occurred because many victims were found long after they were killed. Many bodies were dismembered, two victims were never found, and one victim's identity remains anonymous. In 1991, he committed five murders. The next year he committed eight murders, mostly using strangulation. In 1993, he would commit three more homicides.

## Capture

Rifkin's last victim was a 22-year-old woman named Tiffany Bresciani. He murdered her on June 24, 1993. Rifkin was in his mother's car when he killed her, so he put the body in a tarp, wrapped rope around it, and put it in the trunk. When he arrived home, his mother demanded the car keys because she wanted to go shopping. He gave them to her and she took the vehicle and drove around shopping with the dead body in the trunk. Upon his mother's return, Rifkin moved the body to the garage in a wheelbarrow, eventually moving it to his Mazda pickup truck right before he went out on June 28. As he was driving to Melville's Republic Airport around 3 AM, the state police attempted to pull him over because his front license plate was missing. Rifkin led the police on a high-speed chase and crashed into a utility pole. The police arrested him and found the body in the bed of the truck. When they asked Rifkin who the person was, he indicated that it was a prostitute who he killed and he was headed to the airport to get rid of the body. He then asked the officers if he needed a lawyer.

## His Conviction, Sentence, and Death

Rifkin was interrogated for eight hours, but the police did not record the sessions. Rifkin claimed that he asked for a lawyer at least 20 times and the police refused. The police claim that Rifkin was offered an attorney but declined. Rifkin confessed to 17 murders and even drew maps for the police. The police stopped by Rifkin's mother's home, where Rifkin lived, and talked to his mother. After this she called the attorney, who called the state police and told them to stop interrogating Rifkin, but they did not discontinue their questioning.

On May 9, 1994, after being tried for the murder of Tiffany Bresciani, Rifkin was convicted of murder and reckless endangerment (for the police chase). Later, he pleads guilty to other murders. Altogether, he would get 203 years to life, making him eligible for parole in 2197.

## Rifkin's Mental Health and Personality Characteristics

Rifkin killed because he entertained powerful fantasies about sex. He had taken 228 items from the victims, storing the souvenirs in his room. There were items like jewelry, driver's licenses, and medication bottles. Many sexual domination serial killers use items like this to re-create the feeling they had while they were committing the murder.

Let's take a look at his potential personality profile:

### FFM Personality Profile for Joel Rifkin

| | HIGH | MID | LOW |
|---|---|---|---|
| Openness to experience | ✔ | | |
| Conscientiousness | | ✔ | ✔ |
| Extraversion | | | ✔ |
| Agreeableness | | | ✔ |
| Neuroticism | | | ✔ |

## Openness to Experience: High

Rifkin was intellectually curious, heavily engaged in fantasy (albeit destructive fantasy), and creative (e.g. interest in photography).

## Conscientiousness: Low to Midrange

He didn't always plan things through, for example he was pulled over because he was missing a front license plate on his pickup truck.

## Extraversion: Extremely Low

Rifkin was analytical and shy. He was not talkative, outgoing, assertive, or particularly friendly; however, some sensation-seeking was evident.

## Agreeableness: Low

His level of trust, empathy, humility, straightforwardness, altruism and compliance were generally on the lower side.

## Neuroticism: Low

Rifkin was calm under pressure, but had difficulty regulating anger and could not resist temptations.

## Analysis

Like most if not all serial killers, Rifkin's behavior aligned with certain characteristics of psychopathy; however, the alignment varies from what is typically observed. From the side of primary psychopathy, Rifkin was not particularly manipulative or in possession of superficial charm, but he was somewhat grandiose and he did regularly tell lies. The alignment with secondary psychopathy appears to be stronger, as evidenced by his excitement seeking, parasitic lifestyle, lack of long-term goals, as well as his impulsive and irresponsible tendencies.

Even though some have argued that Rifkin's behavior appears to align with the seven symptom criteria seen in the definition of antisocial personality disorder, he did not have symptoms of conduct disorder before the age of 15. This leaves us with an unusual situation where his behavior seems to align with a personality disorder, but the pattern does not extend from his childhood. Because there is technically no such thing as a late onset personality disorder, this represents a confusing pattern. One that is quite similar to what we see with Ted Kaczynski, who also had extremely low extraversion.

As is the case with many serial killers who go to trial, there was a debate between psychosis and personality pathology in Rifkin's case. The mental health professionals for the defense and the prosecution rendered assessments that fell within the traditional lines, with the defense experts indicating psychosis and the prosecution experts disagreeing. Supporting the case for psychosis, he had told stories about how he would speak to the bodies and how whispers told him to commit the murders.

A mental health professional working for the defense said that Rifkin was the most pathological person she had seen in 20 years, ultimately concluding that he had paranoid schizophrenia. Experts for the prosecution concluded that Rifkin was mentally ill but not insane and that he knew exactly what he was doing. The difficulty with these types of cases is there is no way to be sure that any specific person is or is not psychotic. If Rifkin was not psychotic, is there another explanation for his behavior?

Narcissism may have partially contributed to Rifkin's development into a serial killer. Rifkin endured both verbal and physical bullying during his time in elementary school and high school. It was a significant level of abuse. He could not meet his need to be liked, or to find acceptance among his peers. Due to this, narcissism may have formed and become protective, which is one of the popular conceptualizations of how narcissism functions. The ego finds a way to satisfy its needs and an expansive and satisfying fantasy world is constructed. This probably would not have been problematic alone, but in the case of Rifkin there was little supervision. He was allowed to delve into true crime and repeatedly watch a movie about a serial killer, enabling him to get closer and closer to the fantasy, and blur the line between fantasy and reality. His father's death only increased Rifkin's freedom to explore his fantasies without hardly any supervision and added more pain to his life, therefore more strongly activating his narcissism.

## Conclusion

Rifkin admired Gary Ridgway and would target a similar population, namely prostitutes. Even though Rifkin may have attempted to emulate Ridgway, from a personality point of view, they were quite different. Ridgway was much higher in conscientiousness and extraversion as well as having superficial charm and being manipulative.

Rifkin's unusually high openness and low extraversion demonstrated another mechanism through which sexual domination serial homicide can operate.

# CHAPTER 11

# Danny Rolling: Gainesville Ripper

## Low Conscientiousness—High Neuroticism

Serial killers are sometimes the topics of nightmares and exemplifying this idea better than most is Danny Rolling, otherwise known as the Gainesville Ripper. This emotionally reactive killer inspired the 1996 movie *Scream*.

## Background of Danny Rolling

Daniel Rolling was born on May 26, 1954 in Shreveport, Louisiana. His mother Claudia, was 19 and his father, James, was a police officer and a decorated Korean War veteran. It is believed his father may have had PTSD from his experiences in combat.

Rolling's early years were filled with many horrible and traumatic experiences. James mistreated Rolling as well as Claudia and Rolling's younger brother Kevin, with the level of violence intensifying after Kevin was born. James refused to show affection to Rolling believing that it was not masculine behavior. Claudia left James in 1958 for six weeks but returned to him after he pleaded with her to come back. In 1962, Claudia left James again, and again they would reunite, after which they would move to Shreveport, Louisiana. In 1963, Rolling would fail third grade due to attendance problems. Counselors at the school said that Rolling was suffering from an inferiority complex with aggressive tendencies and poor impulse control.

They indicated that Rolling needed counseling, but he never received it.

Rolling's mother was abused for many years, eventually having what was characterized as a nervous breakdown. Claudia left twice in 1964 and once in 1965, returning each time a few weeks later, which exemplifies a pattern often seen with intimate partner violence. In 1965, Rolling was now 11 years old, and witnesses a fight between Claudia and James. Claudia causes self-inflicted wounds with a razor and locks herself in the bathroom. James broke the bathroom door down and Claudia was hospitalized. Rolling interfered in his father's attack of his mother and was beaten. The same year, Rolling begins to have a number of fantasies about being violent and sadistic and he starts drinking alcohol.

The stress in the Rolling family intensified during the mid-1960's. In 1966, James attempted to kill Claudia. Sometime after, Rolling ran away after being put in jail for two weeks after he was found drinking, but he returned when he became hungry. In 1968, Rolling was looking through a neighbor's bathroom window when James caught and beat him. On Christmas Day 1969, Rolling who was now 15, received a guitar and taught himself to play, which he recalled later as one of the best memories of his life. Rolling would claim that around this same time, he started developing multiple personalities in order to cope with the trauma he was enduring.

## Rolling's Criminal Career

**1970**

In 1970, Rolling went to jail again after being caught drinking by James and was arrested for drinking again in 1971. Later that year Rolling, who had already dropped out of high school, tried to enlist in the Navy but failed the enlistment test. He then joined the Air Force and was stationed in Florida. Rolling would not last long in the Air Force as he was arrested for disobeying orders and drug possession. A mental health professional diagnosed him with a personality disorder. He was kicked out of the Air Force, but allowed to receive an honorable discharge. After this, he went to live with his grandfather and started attending church, evidently becoming quite active in the church community.

### 1974-77
Rolling would get married in September of 1974 and have a daughter in 1975. His wife became increasingly afraid of him as he frequently threatened her. In 1976, a police officer saw Rolling looking through a window of another house and transported him home without arresting him. Rolling and his wife started to have more problems. She had an affair and he became more violent. In 1977, she filed for separation and the couple would divorce six months later. After this, Rolling commits his first sexual assault against a woman who looked like his wife. This would become part of a larger pattern of behavior.

## His Convictions and Sentences

### 1978-79
In 1978 and 1979 we see that Rolling started committing a number of armed robberies. He was arrested and sentenced to six years in prison. Rolling had a turbulent time in the prison system. During his first sentence, he was convicted again of another robbery in Alabama, therefore he had sentences in two jurisdictions. He tried to escape three different times; one of those times it took the police three days to catch him.

### 1984-90
Rolling was released from prison in Alabama in June 1984, but would not take him long to resume criminal activity. He broke into a woman's house in November with the intent of raping her, but he felt badly about it and did not follow through.

At this point, he started traveling around the country committing a number of robberies. He was arrested for one of those robberies and sentenced to four years in 1986. After being released in 1988 he returned to Shreveport, Louisiana, because it was a condition of his release. He found a job there in a restaurant but was fired for missing too much work. On the same day he was fired, he forced his way into a house and murdered a 55-year-old man, a 24-year-old female, and an eight-year-old male, demonstrating a high level of emotional reactivity.

On Christmas Eve, 1989, Rolling broke into a house intent on raping a woman that he had seen before through her window. The woman did not come back to the house, so Rolling left after stealing property, including a .38 caliber revolver.

In May of 1990, Rolling got into a fight with his father, shooting him in the stomach and in the head. James survived but lost use of an eye and an ear. Rolling then committed a number of armed robberies before moving to Florida and assuming the identity Michael Kennedy, Jr. He started camping in the woods behind the University of Florida.

On August 24, 1990, Rolling entered the apartment of two 17-year-old female college students armed with a semiautomatic pistol and a Marine Corps Ka Bar knife. He found one victim asleep downstairs and another upstairs. He attacked the woman upstairs first, raping her and stabbing her to death, before doing the same thing to the victim downstairs. He posed the bodies and showered before leaving.

The next day he used a knife and a screwdriver to pry open a sliding glass door to an apartment of an 18-year-old female. The woman was not home at the time and Rolling waited for her to return. When she did so around 11 AM, he raped her and stabbed her to death. He severed the victim's head and put it on a shelf overlooking her body, which was on the bed.

Two days later, August 27, Rolling attacks two 23-year-old college students, a man and a woman. He made entry into the apartment through the sliding glass door and killed the man.

The woman heard the attack and went to investigate. After encountering Rolling, she tried to barricade herself in one of the bedrooms, but Rolling was able to break through the door. He raped her and stabbed her to death. Rolling left the area and the police assembled a task force to catch the killer.

The police soon identified a suspect, a University of Florida student named Edward Humphrey, who had bipolar disorder and a number of scars on his face from a motor vehicle accident. Shortly after, the police realized the suspect was not the killer, but not before wasting valuable time investigating an innocent man.

## Final Arrest, Conviction, and Sentence

Rolling robbed a grocery store using a firearm in Ocala, Florida. As he was trying to escape, he crashed his vehicle and was arrested. By October 1991, Rolling would be sentenced to three life terms plus 170 years for several burglaries that he committed. In November, he was charged with the Gainesville, Florida murders when DNA and other evidence connected him to those crimes.

In 1992, he was sentenced to another life term plus 30 years for a bank robbery. That same year he started corresponding with Sondra London, who would write a book about him. They announced their engagement in February of 1993.

Rolling initially pleaded not guilty, but changed his plea to guilty against the advice of his attorney on February 15, 1994, the day his trial was scheduled to start. He claimed that he did not want to face the jury as they looked at the crime scene photographs. This is a very unusual move as the prosecution was not offering a deal. Rolling had nothing to lose by going to trial.

The penalty phase continued as it would if he was found guilty by a jury. There were a number of aggravating and mitigating circumstances considered in this case. Aggravating factors include the fact that he was convicted of a number of violent felonies prior to the murders, he was engaged in the commission of other felonies while committing the murders, and the murders were heinous and premeditated. Mitigating factors include the fact that his emotional age was 15, he committed the crimes while under the influence of extreme mental disturbance, he had suffered emotional and physical harm during his childhood, he cooperated with law enforcement and pleaded guilty on all counts, he claimed to have remorse for his actions, he had a family history of mental illness, and his ability to conform his conduct to the requirements of the law was impaired due to mental illness.

After weighing both the aggravating and mitigating factors, the jury sentenced him to death on April 20, 1994. He appealed his sentence all the way to the Florida Supreme Court where his appeal was denied. As he was awaiting his execution he pleaded guilty to three murders he committed in November of 1989.

Rolling was executed by lethal injection on October 25, 2006, at age 52. He sang for a few minutes, but did not apologize.

## Mental Health and Personality Factors for Danny Rolling

Prior to his trial, Rolling was diagnosed with borderline personality disorder, antisocial personality disorder, and paraphilia. His behavior aligns with several characteristics of psychopathy including grandiosity, superficial charm, a tendency to manipulate, a lack of empathy, sensation seeking, impulsivity, irresponsibility

Let's take a look at his potential personality profile:

## FFM Personality Profile for Danny Rolling

|  | HIGH | MID | LOW |
|---|:---:|:---:|:---:|
| Openness to experience | ✔ | | |
| Conscientiousness | | | ✔ |
| Extraversion | | ✔ | |
| Agreeableness | | | ✔ |
| Neuroticism | ✔ | | |

## Openness to Experience: High

Like many serial killers, Rolling had a lot of fantasies, albeit of a destructive nature. He has appreciation for the arts, namely music, and was intellectually curious.

## Conscientiousness: Extremely Low

He was not organized and had very little self-discipline.

## Extraversion: Midrange

There are not many positive emotions expressed by Rolling, but he was assertive and sensation seeking. Like many serial killers who are high in psychopathy with psychopathy, he seemed friendly and outgoing, but these mannerisms were superficial.

## Agreeableness: Low

He had no empathy, did not follow rules, and was not straight-forward.

## Neuroticism: Extremely High

Rolling was depressed, anxious, vulnerable, angry, and had no ability to postpone gratification.

## Analysis

Considering the psychopathy and other personality characteristics at work in this case, the antisocial personality disorder
diagnosis is not really a surprise; however, is not clear why he
was diagnosed with borderline personality disorder. Assuming
that he endorsed all the symptoms, which of course is unknown, the first two symptoms, frantic efforts to avoid abandonment and unstable relationships, may have been endorsed
based on his relationship with his wife. The other symptoms
seem easier to justify including identity disturbance, impulsivity, suicidal behavior, emotional dysregulation, chronic feelings
of emptiness, anger, paranoid ideation or dissociation. The dissociation may have been based on his self-report. They may
have connected his claims about having multiple personalities
with dissociation.

## Multiple Personalities

During the penalty phase, all the experts said he did not have
multiple personalities even though he claimed that an evil persona took control of his mind. What is surprising is that even
the defense expert was able to identify another persona even
under hypnosis. Often in these trials, there is this sense that the
prosecution experts say something biased in favor of the prosecution and the defense does the same thing in favor of the
defense. Therefore, when a defense mental health expert does
not support the defendant's story, it indicates that Rolling may
have been lying.

The case of Danny Rolling supports the idea that serial
killers are created by maltreatment and because they develop a
dysfunctional way of relating to women. This case also high-
lights yet another danger of domestic violence: there are many
victims created by this type of crime. During his series of murders starting in August 1990 in Florida, with the exception of

the one male victim, all of his victims were white petite females with brown hair and brown eyes, which matched the physical profile of his ex-wife. He had stalked each of them, selecting them carefully. His attacks were not random.

The object of Rolling's rage was not women in general; rather, he was acting out a fantasy against women with certain physical characteristics. Almost like he was trying to get revenge against one specific woman by killing other women who had similar characteristics.

## Similarities and Differences to Other Serial Killers

Rolling was a little bit like Ted Bundy in that way and because both had escaped custody. There are more similarities between Rolling and other serial killers beyond the connection to Ted Bundy. Rolling had a history of maltreatment, substance use, and criminal behavior when he was very young, like Carl Panzram (who also escaped from custody). His behavior was similar to the disorganization, sheer violence, and substance use evident with Richard Ramirez. He used the tactic of claiming to have multiple personalities just like Kenneth Bianchi. He was active in a church community for quite some time like Dennis Rader. There is a pattern of escalation similar to that of James DeAngelo. In a way, Rolling was a less disciplined and less organized version of DeAngelo.

## Conclusion

Rolling's life was really a life of horror and in this way, it makes sense it was the inspiration for a horror movie. With his straightforward and violent history, it is not hard to imagine how he developed into the Gainesville Ripper. In the next chapter, we will learn about a killer who was more insidious and, on at least one occasion, was detected through intuition.

# CHAPTER 12

# Rodney Alcala:
# Dating Game Killer

## High Extraversion—Low Neuroticism

Rodney Alcala was known as the Dating Game Killer because he appeared on that television show while active in his serial killing career. Eventually, he would be convicted of seven murders and numerous other crimes. He was active from 1968 to 1979 and likely committed many more murders in addition to those for which he was convicted.

## Background for Rodney Alcala

Alcala was born in 1943 in San Antonio, Texas. His father left the family in 1954 and his mother moved him and his two sisters to Los Angeles, California. In 1960, Alcala joined the Army intending to be a paratrooper but ended up being a clerk instead. Four years later he went absent without leave and hitchhiked from Fort Bragg to Los Angeles. He had what was referred to as a nervous breakdown and was diagnosed with antisocial personality disorder. He was given a medical discharge from the Army. After this, he attended the UCLA School of Arts and Architecture, indicating he may have been high in openness to experience.

## Criminal Career

### 1968

Alcala started his serial killer career on September 25, 1968, at age 25. It was on this day he would target an eight-year-old female victim. He lured her into his car with a photograph of her parents and drove her back to his apartment in Los Angeles. He proceeded to rape her and try to kill her. A witness had followed Alcala's vehicle after seeing the girl get into the car. This witness called the police and when they arrived at Rodney's apartment, he answered the door and said he was getting dressed and he would be with them at a moment. Amazingly, the police courteously waited as Alcala escaped out the back of the apartment. About a minute later the police kicked in the door but were too late to apprehend Alcala.

### 1971-74

Alcala fled to New York City and used an alias to get accepted into New York University, graduating from that school in 1971. In that same year and while still using an alias, Alcala started working in Manhattan as a photographer. Most of the subjects he photographed were young women.

In June 1971, Alcala murdered a 23-year-old woman in her Manhattan apartment. He would not be connected with this crime until much later. The attack on the eight-year-old girl in Los Angeles led to Alcala being added to the FBI's 10 Most Wanted list. When he was working as a counselor at an arts and trauma summer camp in New Hampshire, two of the children at the camp recognized him from a poster hanging in a local post office. Alcala was arrested and extradited to Los Angeles where he would eventually plead guilty to a lesser charge and be given an indeterminate sentence. Alcala would not stay in prison long as he was easily able to manipulate the mental health professionals there. A prison psychiatrist would recommend his release in August 1974.

### 1977

Within a month of his release, Alcala was working as a photographer in Los Angeles. By October, he would be arrested again, this time for kidnapping a 13-year-old female and selling marijuana. He was returned to prison and would be released in June 1977. Evidently, he impressed the prison officials with what they believed was significant improvement. He asked his parole officer for permission to travel to New York and was granted his request. In July 1977, Alcala murdered a 23-year-old woman in New York City. Her name was Ellen Jane Hover and she was the goddaughter of both Dean Martin and Sammy Davis Jr.

By September 1977, Alcala would be working as a typesetter for the Los Angeles Times. In October of that year, he murdered a 19-year-old woman in San Francisco. He was never convicted for this crime. In November he killed an 18-year-old female in Hollywood Hills, strangling her with a pair of pants and beating her. The next month, Alcala committed a home invasion in Malibu where he murdered a 27-year-old woman by strangling her and bludgeoning her with a hammer.

### 1978-79

In September 1978, Alcala appeared as bachelor number one on a dating game television show. He was introduced as a skydiver and photographer who rode motorcycles. Amazingly, Alcala used his real name to get on the show, pointing out a flaw in the research talent of the production staff (he had been on the FBI's Most Wanted list). The female contestant who was directing questions to the bachelors was named Cheryl Bradshaw. She selected Alcala as the winner, meaning her prize was to go on a date with him. The two would interact backstage briefly and later Bradshaw said that she started to feel ill because he was acting creepy. She turned down his offer as she did not want to see him again. Bachelor number two, an actor named Jed Mills, also reported a negative interaction with Alcala. Mills said that Alcala confronted him and said that he would always get the girl.

About five months after this in February of 1979, Alcala,

now 36 years old, raped and choked a 15-year-old girl. This victim escaped when Alcala went into a gas station bathroom and Alcala was arrested. In June, Alcala would commit two more murders. He strangled a 21-year-old woman in a Burbank home invasion and killed a 12-year-old girl named Robin Samso six days later. A witness who saw Samso being dragged to the woods by Alcala, initially did not call the police, but she would soon after that.

## Arrest, Conviction, and Sentence

In July of 1979, Alcala was arrested on suspicion of murdering Robin Samso.

His trial began in March 1980, by April he was convicted of murder and kidnapping. In June, he would be sentenced to death. While he was appealing his death sentence, he was convicted of other crimes. Eventually, his murder conviction was overturned. He was retried for the murder of Robin Sansone in April 1981 and found guilty the next month. In June 1986, he was once again sentenced to death. Incredibly, in 2001 the conviction was overturned again. Alcala was found guilty in 2010 for the murders of Robin Samso and other women and in 2013 he would plead guilty to two more murders.

Even though Alcala was convicted of seven murders, it is suspected he may have killed over 100 women, including victims in Washington and Wyoming.

## Characteristics of Rodney Alcala

Alcala's behaviors align in many ways with the characteristics of primary psychopathy and he has a few that appear to align with secondary psychopathy.

## Primary Psychopathy

He demonstrated a great deal of superficial charm and pathological lying across many domains, including in mental health and forensic settings. He was able to fool mental health professionals in prison, which is surprising given that group is typically well-prepared to deal with psychopathy. Much of the time in prison settings, mental health professionals are considered too skeptical, cynical, and cold. They are typically unwilling to believe even reasonable narratives presented by prisoners. In the case of Alcala, they seemed all too willing to believe his dubious story of reform. It's one thing for mental health professionals, who by training are taught to think in shades of gray, but Alcala also manipulated his parole officer into allowing him to travel to New York where Alcala committed another murder.

Parole officers are typically highly suspect of unusual requests by convicted felons. The most amazing feat of manipulation that Alcala pulled off arguably was when he told police officers, who were responding to a report of a girl's abduction, that he would be with them in a minute and fled out the back door of his apartment. Interestingly, Alcala did not have success trying to manipulate Cheryl Bradshaw on the dating game show. Her intuition about Alcala was dead on and likely saved her life from a serial killer. She was able to pick up on something that mental health professionals in law enforcement repeatedly missed.

Alcala demonstrated low neuroticism, another characteristic of primary psychopathy, when he murdered a high-profile individual, Ellen Jane Hover, even though that behavior generates a greater risk of attracting substantial attention from law enforcement. The Hillside Stranglers, Kenneth Bianchi and Angela Buono, once approached Catharine Baker, who was the daughter of the actor Peter Lorre. The pair were impersonating police officers at the time and they asked for identification. When they saw a picture of her sitting on her father's lap, they realized who she was and let her go, too afraid that her murder would initiate a manhunt that would lead to their arrest.

Alcala did not seem to recognize risks in that same way.

This is also apparent when he signed up to be on a nationally televised game show using his real name. He did not panic in a number of stressful situations in which he placed himself and was consistently reckless.

A look at Alcala's behavior also reveals grandiosity, lack of remorse, and a failure to take responsibility. Alcala's grandiosity was on full display when he acted as his own attorney in his 2010 trial. There was no legal benefit to this; on the contrary, this is typically considered an extremely inadvisable tactic. It did, however, place him as the center of attention in the courtroom and, for a time, let him feel powerful. Alcala never demonstrated any substantial regret or remorse for any of the murders he committed and he never accepted responsibility in any meaningful way.

## Secondary Psychopathy

As far as secondary psychopathy, his behavior aligns with excitement-seeking, impulsivity, and irresponsibility. Sensation seeking preferences were revealed in his desire to be a paratrooper in the Army, his interest in skydiving, and his reference to riding motorcycles. Alcala was exceedingly impulsive in both criminal and noncriminal circumstances, something that is consistent with low conscientiousness and low neuroticism. His irresponsibility was evident in just about every dimension of his life.

Three diagnoses were assigned to Rodney Alcala by various mental health professionals: antisocial personality disorder, narcissistic personality disorder, and borderline personality disorder. The antisocial personality disorder diagnosis is not surprising given the alignment between his behaviors and secondary psychopathy. Similarly, the diagnosis of narcissistic personality disorder would not be seen as unusual because of the alignment between his behavior and primary psychopathy.

The diagnosis that doesn't necessarily seem to fit in an obvious way when compared to his behavior would be borderline personality disorder.

## Borderline Personality Disorder

Let us take a look at the symptoms associated with borderline personality disorder. Borderline personality disorder has nine symptoms, five or more of which must be endorsed for diagnosis.

1. Frantic efforts to avoid abandonment
2. Unstable relationship pattern
3. Unstable self-image
4. Impulsivity in a manner that can cause self-harm
5. Suicidal behavior
6. Emotional dysregulation
7. Persistent feelings of emptiness
8. Substantial anger
9. Paranoid ideation related to stress or severe dissociation

From the information available to the public about this case, there does not appear to be a clear alignment between this disorder and Rodney Alcala's behavior. But it's important to keep in mind that the mental health professionals who came up with this diagnosis were able to assess Alcala in person, and therefore they have a much better perspective and were no doubt given access to information that is not available to the public.

## Antisocial Personality Disorder

The last confusing issue with Rodney Alcala's mental health is the nervous breakdown that was reported in 1964. The term *nervous breakdown* can mean a lot of things, as it is nonspecific.

It can mean something like depression, schizophrenia, bipolar, personality disorders, although the term has the strongest association with adjustment disorder. It is interesting that when presented with Rodney's behavior, the Army mental health professionals decided on antisocial personality disorder. Although that disorder seems to make sense in light of the information presented during the trials, antisocial personality disorder symptoms do not typically overlap with the symptoms normally associated with the term *nervous breakdown*.

Typically, the antisocial personality disorder diagnosis is one that professionals are particularly careful about assigning because there is a significant stigma associated with it, even back in 1964. There may have been other information presented at that time that more clearly connected to antisocial personality disorder or Alcala could have been experiencing something like psychosis or had other symptoms that the mental health professionals did not want to fully explore; therefore, they simply use the term *nervous breakdown*.

When contemplating a potential personality profile for Rodney Alcala, his high levels of extraversion and low neuroticism stand out:

### FFM Personality Profile for Rodney Alcala

|  | HIGH | MID | LOW |
|---|:---:|:---:|:---:|
| Openness to experience | ✔ | | |
| Conscientiousness | | | ✔ |
| Extraversion | | ✔ | |
| Agreeableness | | | ✔ |
| Neuroticism | ✔ | | |

## Openness to Experience: High

Had a pronounced interest in artistic endeavors, one that persisted for many years across several domains, including photography.

## Conscientiousness: Low

Poor work ethic, irresponsible, impulsive.

## Extraversion: High

Charming, manipulative, fearless, dominant, assertive, sensation seeking, comfortable in social situations.

## Agreeableness: Low

Lack of empathy, not straightforward.

## Neuroticism: Low

Calm under extreme stress, not particularly self-conscious, depressed, or anxious.

## Conclusion

Rodney Alcala's case stands as a reminder that mental health professionals should not be too eager to dismiss the value of intuition. The *Dating Game* contestant who selected Alcala only to reject him, sensed something that the professionals missed.

It is not always clear where intuition comes from, but one theory is that it is a combination of unusual stimuli that are processed quite rapidly. She could have observed the way Alcala stared, how he pushed the conversation toward sex, or other nonverbal or verbal cues that somehow when placed together, or perhaps even individually, were perceived as dangerous. It pays to look for an explanation for unexpected circumstances, instead of just assuming the best in anyone who a person happens to encounter.

# CHAPTER 13

# James DeAngelo: Golden State Killer

## High Conscientiousness—Low Agreeableness

James DeAngelo is notable as a serial killer due to his pattern of escalation which manifested over the course of many years, starting out as burglary, moving to rape, and ending with murder. His high conscientiousness facilitated him in being careful not to leave evidence behind and his low agreeableness expressed as a sadistic rage. He never would have been brought to justice, except for the use of a new identification strategy based on matching the DNA from the crime scenes to people that are relatives to the person who left the DNA behind and then working down the family tree to identify the suspect.

## Background of James DeAngelo

James DeAngelo was born in Bath, New York on November 8, 1945, the oldest of four children. DeAngelo's father was an airman in the U.S. Army and because of this, the family moved around quite a bit. Some believe he was in the Air Force, but at the beginning of his service in World War II, the Air Force was not a separate branch of the military. At that time, it was referred to as the United States Army Air Forces, not changing to the Air Force until later in his career. It was reported that DeAngelo's father was physically abusive to his mother, striking her frequently. It would stand to reason that DeAngelo and his siblings were also victims of abuse at the hands of his father.

DeAngelo would earn his GED (a diploma equivalent to a high school diploma) in 1964 and that same year he would join the U.S. Navy, serving for 22 months during the Vietnam War. In 1968, he attended Sierra College in Rocklin, California, and would graduate with an associate's degree in police science. In 1970, he was engaged to a woman named Bonnie Jean Colwell, but she broke off the engagement.

Colwell would later describe DeAngelo's interest in sex as insatiable, saying that it would last for hours and he would listen to The Doors the entire time. Later one victim heard him yelling "I hate you Bonnie" as he was attacking her. Sometime around May of 1973, after a police internship, he became a police officer in Exeter, California, working on the burglary unit, an experience that he undoubtedly used in his criminal career. DeAngelo returned to college, this time at Sacramento State University, where he would earn a bachelor's degree in criminal justice.

DeAngelo would marry Sharon Marie Huddle in November of 1973 and they would live in Citrus Heights, California. The couple had three daughters together and separated in 1991, but Huddle would not file for divorce until 2018. DeAngelo continued working as a police officer, first in Exeter until 1976 and then in Auburn until 1979.

## The Criminal Trajectory of James DeAngelo

### 1975

He was arrested for shoplifting and sentenced to six months of probation in 1979, which ended his career as a police officer. It was reported he attempted to steal a can of dog repellent and a hammer from a drugstore. When store security apprehended him, he feigned a heart attack, something that would be brought up by the prosecution at his bail hearing in 2020. He would be arrested again in 1996 for an incident that occurred at a gas station, but the charges were dropped.

DeAngelo's work history from 1979 through the late 1980s is a bit of a mystery. From the late 1980s until 2017, he worked at a distribution center for a supermarket chain as a truck mechanic. Outside of the shoplifting charge, DeAngelo started his criminal career in April of 1974. Initially, he would be known as the Visalia Ransacker. He committed one homicide and about 120 burglaries in this area of California until December 1975.

### 1976-78

In June of 1976, he became active again, this time in the Sacramento area, where he had recently moved. He would become known as the East Area Rapist (and the East Side Rapist). He committed about 50 separate rapes, the last one taking place in July of 1979.

There were several behaviors that we see across several attacks during this time. DeAngelo would often stalk victims for some time before carrying out an attack. He would burglarize the house in advance sometimes and set it up for a later crime. For example, he would remove the cartridges from firearms, hide shoelaces that he would use to tie up the victims later on, and unlock windows. Even still, the majority the time he pried open a window or door.

Initially, he seemed to target women who were alone and eventually started attacking couples, typically breaking in, threatening them with a firearm, and having the female tie up the male before DeAngelo would tie her up. He would then stack dishes on top of the male's back, saying that if he heard any of the dishes fall, he would kill everybody in the house. After this, he would rape and sodomize the female and sometimes would linger around in the home for hours. Typically, he would steal items that had little monetary value (sometimes these items are called *souvenirs*, this a common behavior for serial killers). He also killed a couple that he confronted in the street in February of 1978.

**1979-86**

DeAngelo resumed activity in October of 1979. This time he would be called the Original Night Stalker and his crimes would take place in several counties in California, including Santa Barbara, Ventura, and Orange. His first crime was tying up a couple after breaking into their home. When the female victim screamed, he fled the scene on a bicycle.

From December of 1979 through July of 1981, DeAngelo would kill nine more people—four couples and one individual. Almost five years later in May of 1986, he would kill a woman in Irvine, California. He sexually assaulted all the female victims before committing murder.

## Arrest, Conviction, and Sentence

The police took quite some time to realize that the same perpetrator committed the crimes in the Sacramento area and the Santa Barbara area. They arrested three different people for DeAngelo's crimes. All three were eventually cleared and DeAngelo was arrested in April of 2018 and was initially charged with eight counts of first-degree murder with special circumstances.

They caught DeAngelo using family DNA. They matched the DNA collected at the crime scenes to somewhere between 10 and 20 people who had the same great-great-great-grandparents as the killer. They were able to narrow down the number of suspects to two using a family tree. One of them was ruled out by a relative's DNA test, leaving just James DeAngelo.

DeAngelo confessed to the murders saying that he was essentially possessed by another personality. In March of 2020, as part of a plea deal to avoid the death penalty, DeAngelo pled guilty to 13 murders and many other charges.

In August 2020, DeAngelo was sentenced to life in prison without the possibility of parole.

## Golden State Killer Characteristics

Let's start by taking a look at James DeAngelo's potential personality profile:

| FFM Personality Profile for James DeAngelo | | | |
|---|---|---|---|
| | HIGH | MID | LOW |
| Openness to experience | | ✔ | |
| Conscientiousness | ✔ | | |
| Extraversion | | ✔ | |
| Agreeableness | | | ✔ |
| Neuroticism | | ✔ | |

## Openness to Experience: Midrange

As is the case with many serial killers, information related to openness to experience is difficult to locate. There are no reports indicating he is particularly high or low in this trait.

## Conscientiousness: High

DeAngelo maintained a job through most of his criminal career, and was quite cautious, successfully evading arrest for many years.

## Extraversion: Midrange

For the most part, it appears as though DeAngelo stayed to himself, although he could be assertive and sensation seeking.

## Agreeableness: Low

DeAngelo is one of the most horrific, heinous, and sadistic serial killers, who demonstrated no empathy and no altruism.

## Neuroticism: Midrange

Like many serial killers, DeAngelo had both low and high scores on various facets of neuroticism. He had difficulty resisting temptation and anger, but he did not appear to be particularly depressed or anxious. He had the ability to engage in high-stress activities without breaking down.

## Analysis

Many people who knew James DeAngelo offered their thoughts about him. He was described as a good father who looked forward to retirement, planned to do a lot of fishing, had perfectly cut grass, and would apologize when overheard cursing. Neighbors also observed his tendency to enter fits of rage, yelling at nothing in his backyard as he paced in circles. One neighbor reported he threatened to deliver a "load of death" if their family dog would not stop barking. He was described as plastic, fake, unwilling to talk about his feelings and someone who would have a temper tantrum if he couldn't find his keys.

## Emotionally Reactive

Even though James DeAngelo had reactive anger, he could keep control of his emotions at certain times. James DeAngelo surrendered without incident when confronted by the police and told officers that he had a roast in the oven when they informed him that he was being charged with several murders. This seems to point to the idea that he was not emotionally reactive.

It has been suspected that DeAngelo made several calls to police and to victims specifically to taunt them. People claiming to be the perpetrator could have made these calls, so there is no way to be certain, but victims did believe that the voice on the phone matched the perpetrator; therefore, it seems likely that DeAngelo made at least some of these calls.

Many involved in the case have entered their opinions

about DeAngelo's mental health. A prosecutor in the case described him as a cruel, intelligent, and sadistic killer as well as a sociopath and master manipulator. There are strong suspicions by many that DeAngelo faked having delusions and hallucinations when he talked about that other personality that drove him to kill, and that in reality, he has personality pathology.

## Comparison to Other Serial Killers

DeAngelo stands out among serial killers several reasons. He mostly operated within three narrow roles spanning from 1974 to 1986, although he committed just one murder in 1986 after waiting five years. Factoring that particular murder out of the equation, he was primarily active for a seven-year period (1974–1981). During this time, he functioned as a burglar for a few years, then a rapist, and then a serial killer. There was some overlap, but he mostly kept the roles separate. There was a methodical escalation as he moved toward being a serial killer.

DeAngelo's behavior aligned with psychopathy. For example, he demonstrated:

- no empathy
- no remorse
- high sadism
- a sense of entitlement
- a tendency to be manipulative
- pathological lying
- sensation seeking
- and fearless dominance

There is no convincing evidence that he is delusional. It seems likely he made that up to escape responsibility. Like many serial killers, he was interested in police work, except in his case he was able to get through the screening process to be a police officer. I think the reason he was able to do this is that he did not have a criminal history up to that point. Most people who become serial killers commit crimes when they are young, which he very well may have done, but there is no record of any crimes. Most people who commit shoplifting, as DeAngelo did at least once, often commit shoplifting many times throughout their lives.

Even though DeAngelo did make many mistakes, in general, he planned out his crimes carefully. If it were not for the creative investigation using DNA, he never would have been caught for any of his rapes, murders, and burglaries. His law enforcement experience probably helped him to avoid being identified. His somewhat regimented progression through the different roles probably also helped him to get away with crimes as well. The progression through the stages allowed him to become an efficient burglar, which would be a key part of his future crimes. The uncertainty in the practice of burglary was removed through experience.

## Prolific Criminal

DeAngelo was a prolific criminal, committing somewhere near 200 separate offenses, each one carrying multiple charges if he had been arrested. If he would have been charged for everything he did, over a thousand felonies would have been accumulated. For example, even something like a burglary, there is the actual burglary charge, possession of burglar's tools, possession of a burglar's mask, and possession of a deadly weapon during the commission of a felony. Not all those were separate charges during the time he committed them, but by today's standards, he would be charged with at least those crimes for one burglary.

## Attacking Couples

Another unusual characteristic of James DeAngelo is the fact that he assaulted and killed so many couples during this part of his criminal career. This represents a similarity to David Berkowitz and Richard Ramirez. Berkowitz and Ramirez were disorganized killers; however, DeAngelo mixed the pattern of targeting couples with being organized, which, in one sense, made him even more dangerous.

This behavior is quite rare among serial killers and it seems to be part of the escalation in the case of DeAngelo. He started off attacking individuals and then moved up to attacking couples, which implies that his sadistic drive was not being satisfied with attacking individuals. I think it is probably the case that many serial killers desire to do what DeAngelo did, but they didn't feel confident enough. DeAngelo was a particularly fearless and physically fit killer, who believed he could physically dominate and intimidate victims.

The last unusual item about DeAngelo is the idea that he could have this type of escalation and yet stop. Some people do not believe his last crime was in 1986, so it may have been that he just slowed down, but either way there was a marked change in the frequency of his crimes. It is not clear what happened. Perhaps his drive decreased, he found some other way to satisfy it that was safer, he was no longer physically or emotionally able to commit the crimes, or something else occurred that is to remain unknown.

## Conclusion

DeAngelo is a good example of how horrible someone's behavior can be when they lack empathy, have an abundance of aggression, and have a clear object of hatred at which they can express their aggression.

# CHAPTER 14

# Summary

Sexual domination and other types of serial killers have forged a trail of destruction through various communities. Society would benefit from having some way to identify who would become a serial killer and who would not.

## Early Identification and Intervention

If there were some way to intervene early, it is believed that such intervention could save many lives. As we see from the personality diversity of the select serial killers discussed in this book, there is no combination of personality traits that clearly points toward serial homicide. It could be argued that the serial killers with high conscientiousness, extremely low agreeableness, and low neuroticism may be more dangerous because they are highly organized, think through their crimes carefully, have no empathy, and are extremely calm. They commit the same type of crimes as other serial killers, but their probability of being caught for any given murder is lower.

Even still, there are many examples of serial killers with different personalities who have killed dozens of individuals. There are many serial killers who have never been arrested, and one could only imagine that there is personality diversity among that population as well.

The development of a man into a serial killer is referred to as a low probability event. There have been thousands of accusations made in seriousness, in jest, and casually, identifying people as potential serial killers, but only a very few men will ever actually become this type of homicide offender. A man can have the perfect profile to become a serial killer and go on to commit petty crimes, moderate level crimes, or they may live a life without committing any crimes.

## Identifying Killers Using Personality Theory

Using personality theory to identify killers would cause a false positive epidemic. This type of categorization error occurs when some type of test indicates that a condition is present, but the condition is not present. For example, imagine a test designed to identify students in high school who would be math geniuses in a community that desperately needed mathematicians. The test is designed as a screening tool to identify anybody who could potentially be in the group. Therefore, it returns a positive result in many instances where the student is not actually particularly good at mathematics because the cost of missing a student who may be mathematically inclined is too high.

This type of test would have a high false-positive rate by design. In essence, a positive result just means that teachers should further assess the student to determine if the student is in fact mathematically talented. The test does not provide a definitive result—it only points toward future testing. Perhaps a design like this would be appropriate if the more comprehensive testing was too expensive or prohibitive to administer to a wide group of students.

When contemplating this analogy in light of personality theory, a few problems quickly develop. Imagine a personality test designed to pick up certain extreme scores that could indicate that an individual may be at risk to be a serial killer. Hypothetically, in a population of 1,000 men, perhaps 50 would be identified as appropriate for further assessment. Here is where this model would run into difficulty. There is no further assessment without encroaching on the rights of the individual. Unlike a mathematics test, which most students would not care about taking and would not feel represented an invasion of privacy, most individuals from the general population would not feel comfortable taking an assessment that could potentially identify them as a future serial homicide offender.

## What Use Then is Personality Theory?

As it appears that personality theory has no practical application for spotting future serial killers on a large scale, what use is personality theory in this area? Its primary role would be to assist a potential victim with detecting possible dangerousness in another individual.

A non-negligible proportion of individuals who kill another person do so because of a sexual domination motive, even if the killer never becomes a serial killer. Furthermore, rapists often share the sexual domination motive of serial killers.

Any type of rapist or murderer is dangerous, regardless of how many people they offend against. Therefore, the ability to spot warning signs of sexual domination tendencies has the potential to keep people safer.

Of all the personality traits, which ones should people be on the lookout to identify potentially dangerous persons? Dangerous traits include:

- lack of empathy
- history of violence
- manipulative
- narcissistic
- low neuroticism
- high sensation seeking
- a penchant for aggressive sex
- general hatred of women

An individual can have every characteristic on this list and never commit a crime in his entire life. This list contains the characteristics most indicative of a man who is at risk, at some point in his life, to harm one or more women. Some of the characteristics are so obviously dangerous that anyone interested in protecting themselves would be wary of them automatically, for example, violent history and men who hate women.

Other characteristics are more insidious. Many men are sensation-seeking and not criminal. Similarly, many men are manipulative, but their goals could be to exploit men or women for money, attention, or social status.

If somebody is aware of characteristics associated with increased risk of violence toward women, that may keep them safe from potentially dangerous men who they know, but most serial killers target victims who they do not know. Furthermore, as demonstrated in some of the chapters covering individual serial killers, some killers are not motivated by sexual domination.

How is it that women, or for that matter men, can protect themselves from rage-filled, violent offenders who, from the point of view of potential victims, attack people at random? From a logistical point of view, the same advice that would protect a person from any killer would also be useful to protect them from serial killers. For example, maintaining high situational awareness, always having access to a phone, avoiding being alone in high-risk situations, and having some training in self-defense.

These tips are fairly well known, but what about from a personality point of view? Can understanding the psychology of killers be used to impart some level of protection?

## Protecting Oneself

There is no perfect way to protect oneself, but there is one area that may be somewhat beneficial, namely, the maintenance of boundaries. Killers who target strangers often rely on getting the stranger into a somewhat vulnerable position before striking, which involves a degree of manipulation. When killers do this, they rely on a victim having midrange or high agreeableness; therefore, they are hoping that the victim has a tendency to trust, be altruistic, empathic, and values cooperation. All of these are socially desirable traits, but they can strongly work against a victim in a crisis situation, specifically because the victim does not realize they are in jeopardy.

For example, Ted Bundy was known to wear a fake cast to appear more vulnerable. He would lure women to the back of his car where he could more easily attack them. He also once kidnapped a woman by pretending to be a police officer. Although he had a fake badge, he was driving a Volkswagen Beetle, claiming that it was his undercover vehicle. She had a feeling that something was wrong, but she went with him anyway. Fortunately, in her case, she did manage to escape, but the maintenance of boundaries would have prevented the traumatic experience she had at the hands of Ted Bundy.

## Boundaries

Boundaries are a set of rules that a person defines for themselves internally and expresses externally toward members of society. The set of rules is specific to the situation, for example, a person will have a different set of rules for interacting with their spouse than they will for interacting with a shopper in line with them at the grocery store.

What people find so often is that when they violate the set of rules, something undesirable tends to occur. Perhaps a person loans money to another individual at work who they barely know. A little voice inside the person's head tells them not to trust the other individual, but another voice urges them to be a generous person. The key to maintaining successful boundaries is to maintain them the same way in every situation *without exception*—even when maintaining the boundary seems cold and unfriendly.

The Psychology of Notorious Serial Killers

Killers who are trying to maneuver a victim into a vulnerable situation are counting on that victim to violate boundaries, just as the killer has violated socially acceptable boundaries. If a person encounters another who is deviating from accepted boundaries, this is a reasonable indication that something is amiss. Killers often combine the *superficial charm* that I referred to in earlier chapters with an exorbitant amount of *pressure in the moment* to elicit boundary-breaking behavior in a potential victim. A good example of a tough decision to maintain boundaries is from the Rodney Alcala case, which I talked about in Chapter 12.

He won the *Dating Game,* but the other winning contestant refused to go on a date with him because she sensed something was wrong. There must have been a tremendous amount of pressure on her to simply go on a date with him. After all, she had just won a game that was nationally televised. However, she maintained her boundaries and likely saved her own life from the hands of the notorious Rodney Alcala.

## Why are Serial Killers Fascinating?

Most people realize that the chances of being targeted by a serial killer are remarkably low, even though, of course, the consequences in those rare occasions are tragic. The interest that many people in serial killers and true crime in general, exceeds the impact of criminality in their daily lives. Put another way, there is something fascinating about serial killing that draws people to study it far beyond the proportional necessity to develop strategies to identify serial killers and protect society from these types of offenders.

Many factors lead to this fascination. I will discuss a few specific factors in this final section, namely novelty, brutality, and scope of mission.

146

## Novelty

Often in the course of life, we hear fascinating and compelling claims made by various individuals. For example, claims of people seeing Bigfoot, the Loch Ness Monster, alien spacecraft, and ghosts. People are fascinated with all manner of supernatural and preternatural occurrences, but this fascination often turns to disappointment as the facts do not support many extreme claims.

The novelty of serial killing, however, is not only fascinating but it has been demonstrated repeatedly as a true phenomenon. Serial homicide offenders are real and they have been a scourge to society as long as society has existed. The stories of a single killer who commits dozens of homicides seem impossible, but these offenders have existed and almost certainly will exist in the future. As horrible as they are, the notion of the serial killer gives people an opportunity to study something that appears improbable if not impossible.

## Brutality

The next factor that facilitates interest in these offenders would be the sheer brutality of their crimes. It is only natural to be fascinated with crimes involving disturbing levels of aggression, but serial killers take things to the extreme. They commit these horrible acts repeatedly, sometimes over the course of years. If any particular individual was interested in five or ten different murders that were particularly heinous, it is easy to see why one serial killer would be more interesting than all those cases combine. One serial killer could be responsible for that many crimes or more.

## Scope of Mission

Unlike killers who commit a single homicide, serial killers appear to be on a mission whose purpose deviates from traditional homicide motives. They have a motivation that is rarely personal toward the victim; rather, they are driven from a deep, dark need for sexual domination that originates totally outside the realm of the victim. Their murderous behavior stems from a disrupted childhood, terrible relationships with mother figures, horrible abuse, bullying, as well as disturbing personality features like psychopathy and narcissism.

Traditional murderers are often thought of as having made a mistake in the heat of the moment or looking to obtain or protect wealth. Therefore, their motives are sometimes laced with jealousy, difficulty regulating anger, substance use, and a desire for financial gain. In essence, even though serial killers are substantially more complex than *regular* murderers, their motives and origins are more straightforward and seemingly less under their control. They are predators, who due to circumstances both in and out of their control, have taken on a dangerous mission. Killing is not simply something they did; it is their identity.

## Conclusion

As I bring a close to this discussion and review of serial killing behavior and personality, I hope that readers were able to get something insightful and interesting from this text. Even though any particular person is unlikely to encounter a serial killer in their lifetime, the dangers of sexual domination motives reach far beyond serial homicides.

Every day, and in communities around the world, people struggle with offenders and potential offenders of all types. A personality that drives somebody to exert sexual control can exist anywhere on a continuum, all the way from a person who occasionally thinks of forceful sex but never acts on it, all the way up to a serial rapist and killer.

Mental health counselors work tirelessly to help the victims of these personality types by providing direct services and by continuing research so that we can better understand how certain personality traits and facets contribute to destructive behavior. Counselors attempt to cut through all the speculation and pseudoscience to find the truth. We want to provide the most accurate and useful information to the public and work toward a world without the suffering caused by pathological offenders.

# References

http://www.personal.psu.edu/faculty/j/5/j5j/IPIPNEOdescriptions.html

Ben-Porath, Y. S. (2019). Uses and misuses of Ted Kaczynski's MMPI. Journal of Personality Assessment, 101(2), 117–122. doi:10.1080/00223891.2018.1468337

Butcher, J. N., Hass, G. A., Greene, R. L., Nelson, L. D., Nichols, D. S., & Williams, C. L. (2018). Using the MMPI-2 in Forensic Assessment: Response to Criticism About a Case Study. Journal of Personality Assessment, 1–6. doi:10.1080/00223891.2018.1493488

Glaberson, W. (2004, October 18). The Death Penalty as a Personal Thing. New York Times, 154(53006), B1.

Wardle, C. (2003). The "Unabomber" vs. the "Nail Bomber": a cross-cultural comparison of newspaper coverage of two murder trials. Journalism Studies, 4(2), 239. doi: 10.1080/1461670032000074829

Moen, O. M. (2019). The Unabomber's ethics. Bioethics, 33(2), 223–229. doi: 10.1111/bioe.12494

https://www.fbi.gov/history/famous-cases/unabomber

https://www.history.com/news/unabomber-letter-bombs-investigation-arrest

http://www.karenfranklin.com/files/Kazynski-Johnson_Report-09.11.98.pdf

American Psychiatric Association. (2013). Diagnostic and statistical manual of mental disorders (5th ed.). Arlington, VA: Author.

http://maamodt.asp.radford.edu/Psyc%20405/serial%20killers/Berkowitz,%20David.pdf

https://www.history.com/this-day-in-history/son-of-sam-arrested

https://www.crimemuseum.org/crime-library/serial-killers/david-berkowitz/

https://murderpedia.org/male.B/b/berkowitz.htm

https://time.com/3979004/son-of-sam-caught/

https://www.ariseandshine.org/my-life-story.html

International Business Times. (8 C.E. 2011). Jailed Son of Sam Killer Won't Seek Parole, Says Jesus Set Him Free. International Business Times.

Williams, D. J. (2017). Mephitic projects: a forensic leisure science analysis of the BTK serial murders. Journal of Forensic Psychiatry & Psychology, 28(1), 24–37.

Lynes, A., & Wilson, D. (2015). Driving, Pseudo-reality and the BTK: A Case Study. Journal of Investigative Psychology & Offender Profiling, 12(3), 267–284.

Bartels, R., & Parsons, C. (2009). The Social Construction of a Serial Killer. Feminism & Psychology, 19(2), 267–280. doi:10.1177/0959353509102224

Simons, E. B. (2005). Forensic Computer Investigation Brings Notorious Serial Killer BTK to Justice. Forensic Examiner, 14(4), 55–57

https://www.psychologytoday.com/us/blog/wicked-deeds/201902/inside-the-mind-serial-killer-dennis-rader-aka-btk

https://www.kansas.com/news/special-reports/btk/article1003766.html

https://www.wibw.com/home/headlines/7446541.html

http://maamodt.asp.radford.edu/Psyc%20405/serial%20killers/Rader,%20Dennis%20-%202005.pdf

https://www.thoughtco.com/profile-of-joel-rifkin-973144

https://www.investigationdiscovery.com/crimefeed/crime-history/a-frenzy-of-murder-story-of-new-york-serial-killer-joel-rifkin

Watkin, J. G. (1984). The bianchi (L.A. hillside strangler) case: Sociopath or multiple personality? International Journal of Clinical and Experimental Hypnosis, 32(2), 67–101. doi:10.1080/00207148408416005

Miller, E. (1988). Defining hysterical symptoms1. Psychological Medicine, 18(02), 275. doi:10.1017/s0033291700007820

Kirschner, D. (1992). Understanding Adoptees Who Kill: Dissociation, Patricide, and the Psychodynamics of Adoption. International Journal of Offender Therapy and Comparative Criminology, 36(4), 323–333. doi:10.1177/0306624x9203600406

https://www.psychologytoday.com/us/blog/the-human-equation/201703/split-decisions-in-the-courtroom

# References

https://latimesblogs.latimes.com/lanow/2010/08/hillside-strangler-denied-parole.html

https://www.historylink.org/File/8613

https://www.ibtimes.com/rodney-alcala-dating-game-killer-psychological-profile-2623321

https://healthpsychologyconsultancy.wordpress.com/2012/09/13/856/

https://www.thoughtco.com/profile-of-serial-killer-rodney-alcala-973104

https://murderpedia.org/male.A/a/alcala-rodney.htm

http://maamodt.asp.radford.edu/Psyc%20405/serial%20killers/Alcala.%20Rodney%20_2012_.pdf

https://www.history.com/news/serial-killer-dating-game-rodney-alcala

https://the-line-up.com/rodney-alcala-the-dating-game-killer-victims

Sands, Stella (2011). The Dating Game Killer. New York: St. Martin's Press.

https://abcnews.go.com/US/inside-timeline-crimes-golden-state-killer/story?id=54744307

https://www.refinery29.com/en-us/2020/06/9885795/golden-state-killer-timeline-murders-arrest-trial

https://www.sfgate.com/bayarea/article/east-area-rapist-golden-state-killer-timeline-12863609.php

https://www.biography.com/crime-figure/golden-state-killer#:~:text=Suspect%3A%20Joseph%20DeAngelo&text=He%20spent%20some%20of%20his,Killer%20remembered%20him%20crying%20about.

https://www.washingtonpost.com/news/post-nation/wp/2018/04/26/joseph-deangelo-golden-state-killer-suspect-was-normal-grandpa-according-to-teen/

https://www.buzzfeednews.com/article/skbaer/the-suspected-golden-state-killer-witnessed-two-men-rape

https://heavy.com/news/2018/04/joseph-deangelo-mother-father-kathleen-bosanko/

https://www.sfgate.com/crime/article/Golden-State-Killer-Joseph-DeAngelo-mental-health-15374517.php

https://www.sacbee.com/news/local/crime/article229045029.html

https://www.latimes.com/california/story/2020-06-28/closing-the-golden-state-killer-case-with-a-pending-confession-circus-atmosphere-and-a-bar-of-gold

Silva, J. A., Leong, G. B., & Ferrari, M. M. (2004). A neuropsychiatric developmental model of serial homicidal behavior. Behavioral Sciences & the Law, 22(6), 787–799. doi:10.1002/bsl.620

Murray, J. L. (2016). The Role of Sexual, Sadistic, and Misogynistic Fantasy in Mass and Serial Killing. Deviant Behavior, 38(7), 735–743. doi:10.1080/016396 25.2016.1197669

Brief Treatment and Crisis Intervention 2007 7(1):77-89; doi:10.1093/brief-treatment/mhl021

https://murderpedia.org/male.R/images/ridgway_gary/reports/summary.pdf

https://murderpedia.org/male.R/r/ridgway-gary.htm

https://www.biography.com/news/danny-rolling-scream-killer-gainesville

https://fsulawrc.com/fall/flsupct/83638/83638ini.pdf

http://www.clarkprosecutor.org/html/death/US/rolling1051.htm

https://www.orlandosentinel.com/news/os-xpm-1994-03-18-9403180387-story.html

https://www.youtube.com/watch?v=hDiVAUz5Jyo

https://www.bostonmagazine.com/news/2020/06/23/whitey-bulger-final-days/

https://archive.nytimes.com/www.nytimes.com/interactive/us/bulger-timeline.html#/#time256_7771

https://www.cnn.com/2014/09/17/justice/whitey-bulger-six-things/index.html

https://www.cnn.com/2013/06/12/us/whitey-bulger-fast-facts/index.html

https://abcnews.go.com/Health/whitey-bulger-case-hit-man-denies-serial-killer/story?id=19439411

https://www.mercurynews.com/2020/02/22/after-learning-of-whitey-bulger-lsd-tests-juror-has-regrets/

https://www.newyorker.com/magazine/2015/09/21/assets-and-liabilities

Constable, A., & Goodgame, D. (1985). TAKING A BYTE OUT OF CRIME Police hail computer system that cracked the Night Stalker case. TIME Magazine, 126(15), 96.

International Business Times. (2013, June 7). Richard Ramirez Dies: Complete List And Timeline Of "Night Stalker" Victims [PHOTO]. International Business Times.

https://apnews.com/8d5893ad279d758b655873bc19f2510b

https://www.biography.com/crime-figure/ed-gein

https://allthatsinteresting.com/edward-gein

https://www.britannica.com/biography/Ed-Gein

https://www.history.com/this-day-in-history/real-life-psycho-ed-gein-dies

https://murderpedia.org/male.G/g/gein-edward.htm

http://www.ejumpcut.org/archive/onlinessays/JC43folder/EdGein.html

Schechter, H. (1989). Deviant: The shocking true story of the original "psycho". New York: St. Martin's Paperbacks.

Gollmar, R.H. (1981). America's Most Bizarre Murderer: Edward Gein. New York, NY: Windsor Publishing Co.

Woods, P.A. (1995) Ed Gein: Psycho. St. Martin's Press, NY.

## About the Author

Dr. Todd Grande is a professional counselor, counselor educator, and content creator who specializes in personality disorders, addiction, recovery from trauma, psychopathology, and assessment.

His YouTube channel, *Dr. Todd Grande*, has nearly 700,000 subscribers and is growing rapidly. Dr. Grande covers a wide range of topics including mental health disorders, personality theory, true crime, relationships, and narcissism. He is a Licensed Professional Counselor of Mental Health (LPCMH) and Licensed Chemical Dependency Professional (LCDP) in the State of Delaware and is a National Certified Counselor (NCC). Dr. Grande holds a Master's of Science in Community Counseling from Wilmington University and a Ph.D. in Counselor Education and Supervision from Regent University. For many years, he was an associate professor in Wilmington University's CACREP-accredited Clinical Mental Health Counseling program and provided counseling and consulting services in his local community.

His next book: *Harm Reduction*, a fiction novel
His YouTube channel: Dr. Todd Grande